T0194256

You Are
Dearly Loved

SHEILA S. DEMPSEY, PH.D.

BALBOA.
PRESS
A DIVISION OF HAY HOUSE

Balboa Press books may be ordered through booksellers or by contacting:

Balboa Press
A Division of Hay House
1663 Liberty Drive
Bloomington, IN 47403
www.balboapress.com
1 (877) 407-4847

Because of the dynamic nature of the Internet, any web addresses or
links contained in this book may have changed since publication and
may no longer be valid. The views expressed in this work are solely those
of the author and do not necessarily reflect the views of the publisher,
and the publisher hereby disclaims any responsibility for them.

The author of this book does not dispense medical advice or prescribe the use
of any technique as a form of treatment for physical, emotional, or medical
problems without the advice of a physician, either directly or indirectly. The
intent of the author is only to offer information of a general nature to help
you in your quest for emotional and spiritual well-being. In the event you use
any of the information in this book for yourself, which is your constitutional
right, the author and the publisher assume no responsibility for your actions.

Any people depicted in stock imagery provided by Getty Images are
models, and such images are being used for illustrative purposes only.
Certain stock imagery © Getty Images.

Print information available on the last page.

ISBN: 978-1-9822-1007-6 (sc)
ISBN: 978-1-9822-1009-0 (hc)
ISBN: 978-1-9822-1008-3 (e)

Library of Congress Control Number: 2018909778

Balboa Press rev. date: 01/16/2019

CONTENTS

This book is dedicated to all my fellow beings on earth. I thank you for sharing this incredible journey with me. You are my heroes.

ACKNOWLEDGEMENTS

How
Did the rose
Ever open its heart
And give to this world
All its Beauty?
It felt the encouragement of light
Against its
Being

Hafiz[1]

I offer my deepest gratitude to the following people for sharing their remarkable hearts and minds with me as I wrote this book. They are Lightworkers who are making the world a more beautiful place to live.

First of all I'd like to thank my sister, Dr. Joan Rossi, for her generous and loving emotional support, as well as her invaluable and wise editorial advice. She was always there for me during the writing of this book and I could not have done it without her.

I thank my editor and dear friend, Howard Wells, for his wise, insightful editorial guidance and his generous encouragement of my writing. I thank him for the gift of his patient acceptance of my process even when it was difficult to understand. And I thank him for the many food-for-the-soul conversations that help me to feel more at home in the world.

I thank Hal Zina Bennett for his open-hearted support and expertise when I first began this book as well as later on in the process.

I thank Jan Allegretti for her astute and insightful evaluation of the early manuscript that helped me to focus on what the book was truly about. And I thank her for her loving encouragement of my writing.

I thank my dear friend, Allen Shifrin, for his never-wavering message of needing to trust my own intuition about what felt right for the book, even when he disagreed with me. I thank him for his generous and expert editorial help, and for the stunning beauty of his photography.

I thank my dear friend, Cathy Facciola, for many years of sensitive, loving, and laughter-filled emotional support and her unwavering support of my writing. She gave me consistently incisive advice on all aspects of the book from its inception.

I thank my dear friend, Nancy Hathaway, for her loving and whole-hearted support for the book which gave me confidence to continue to write when I needed it. I thank her for telling me that she'd wept after finishing the manuscript because she'd been touched. I knew I was on the right track.

I thank my dear friend, Lauren Abdelaziz, for her unwavering, unconditional love for me and support for the book. I thank her also for telling me she cried while reading the manuscript, and for reminding me that the world needed its message.

I thank my dear friend, Cindy McWilliams, for her light in my life.

She has always seen the good in me and has always supported my gifts unconditionally, especially the writing of this book.

I thank Jackie M. and her family for their generosity in letting me share their personal story.

INTRODUCTION

Welcome to these pages, dear one, written with love and respect for you, no matter who you are in the eyes of society, no matter what you may have done or neglected to do, or wherever you are in your life's journey. It's my deepest desire to help alleviate suffering—yours—or the suffering of someone close to you, especially if that suffering is an outgrowth of feeling unloved or even unlovable. I've known that feeling very well. It is my heart's desire to help you know and feel that you are dearly loved.

A Little Background

My story begins with a summer afternoon in 1980 when my life was turned upside down. On that day an energy of such immense power and love burst through me that, for the first time in my young adult life, I felt truly loved. In the middle of a life filled with physical and emotional illness, it was a mystical and miraculous moment, and I would never be the same again.

I may not have known love in my early years, but love knew me. As a result of that miraculous moment when time seemed to stop, I discovered that there was an ocean of love holding me in its arms. It was within me already—as it is also within you and embraces you this very moment. Recognizing this love was a matter of changing the focus of my awareness and allowing for possibilities of deeper truths that I could not have even dreamed of before.

I had been an abused child, and by the time I was an adolescent the accumulated traumas had left me with profound, emotional wounds that needed loving attention to heal—loving attention that I would not learn to give myself for many years. I stumbled along in my early life, living in a kind of unconscious fog. Stuck in fear and anger and self-doubt, all of which left me inclined to mistrust others, I was never truly able to love myself or anyone else. Neither was I able to perceive and accept the love of Spirit that I have since come to realize was with me all the while. Awareness of Spirit's love began to unfold that summer day many years ago when that force of pure love flowed over and through me.

There were glimpses in my childhood of the blessings that the future would hold, however. I had these glimpses every time I got up the courage to ask questions and found myself willing to be open to new answers. I remember, as a small child, imploring a priest who was a family friend to bless our little angel, a black and white Beagle-mix named Daisy. He said, no, he couldn't bless Daisy, but he offered to bless my inanimate rosary beads instead. That seemed outrageous and backward to me, even though the very idea of questioning the authority figures of one's religion was close to unthinkable in my home. I let him bless the beads but I was not happy.

There were childhood glimpses of the deep love I would later experience as well. Although my family did the best they could to show love, mostly the glimpses were with the precious nonhumans in my world: Daisy, Sophie (my sweet, tiny, cross-eyed kitten who turned out to be male, but I kept the name anyway), Pokey (the neighbor's dog whose heart really belonged to me), and many other exuberant and amazing creatures who came my way. The pure love that we shared was the closest I came to the force of love I later experienced and came to call divine.

Over the years, the desire to share the experience and the *feeling* of this love continued to grow within me. I felt safe sharing the love with people individually and in small groups as part of my work, but it took a long time to overcome most of the fear of being so exposed and vulnerable in actually sharing my thoughts and feelings with the public. I was living under the illusion that I had to be close to perfect in order to put myself out there, that I had to read another book or attend another seminar so that I didn't miss something I should know. Ultimately, however, the desire to give and to share has been stronger than the fear of being vulnerable and the desire to stay safe. Anaïs Nin said it so well, "And the day came when the risk to remain tight in a bud was more painful than the risk it took to blossom."

Beginner's Mind

I ask that you approach the experience of this book with what Zen calls the Beginner's Mind: a state of mind free of preconceptions and biases. With Beginner's Mind one can say, "I do not know right now, nor do I have to know. I will just observe and be open to whatever arises in this moment." Suzuki Roshi, put it this way, "In the beginner's mind there are many possibilities, in the expert's there are few."[1] If we can be open to possibilities together, one moment at a time, perhaps we can open ourselves to greater insight and grace. We can open to the blessings that the universe wishes to give us.

My own journey with Beginner's Mind has been one that I could not have imagined years ago. If anyone had told me in my teens or twenties that along with the adversity and grief and challenges that life would bring there would be these times of such intense, ecstatic joy that I could hardly stand it, I would have said they were downright mad. But that is what has turned out to be true, and that truth arose out of the fertile ground of not having to know.

What I Share

What I share with you here are my experiences and what I have come to understand—my version of reality. That version of reality has been shaped in part by two graduate degrees: a Ph.D. in psychology, where my interest was focused on lifespan development, and a Masters of Education in counseling. After I finished my formal education I taught a variety of psychology courses at the college level. As fascinating as the many fields of psychology are, though, I always felt that the psychological perspective alone was an incomplete view of life. We are spiritual beings first and foremost and that truth cannot be left out of our education.

I left teaching to spend several years working with a brilliant and creative clinical psychologist in New York, Dr. Andrew Gentile. Under his aegis I had the opportunity to do counseling that incorporated meditation, spirituality, and imagery techniques. Now I do what is referred to as spiritual-intuitive healing work. I don't do the healing myself; rather I act as a conduit for the healing energies of Spirit. As the years have gone by, my focus has increasingly been one of helping people to become aware of how loved they are. It is my hope and my deep desire that this book will give you the courage to open your heart to the love of Spirit.

Interspersed among the stories of my experiences are some of the insights that I have acquired along the way, as well as what I understand of spiritual theory. I offer many things as possibilities, some that may seem outrageous and some that are quite gentle. Please take only what feels right for you—what resonates with you— and leave the rest. I offer it all to you with absolute love.

Spirit's Voice

All of us are capable of quieting the inner chatter and "noise" of our minds in order to hear the still, small voice of Spirit speaking to us. In a way, it's like tuning a radio. We can hear only one station at a time because we can tune in to only one frequency at a time. The different frequencies are all available to us; we just need to do some fine tuning to hear them. The higher frequency of Spirit's voice is also always available to us and represents a higher level of wisdom and universal knowledge. As we go within and quiet our minds, the mind's "receiver" is able to pick up or tune in to this higher frequency.

Through decades of meditating, I have learned how to tune my mind's receiver. I've learned how to distinguish the voice of Spirit from the voice of my own mind. Of course, the voice of Spirit is filtered through my consciousness, but it's still recognizable as a voice distinct from my own. When Spirit is speaking to me or through me there is a certain feeling, a certain unique vibrational force that comes through. It's the energy and feeling of deep peace and compassion for all of life. It's the feeling of having my heart opened and of having my consciousness expanded beyond the usual limits of the material world.

There were times during the writing of this book when I felt that the words being written were coming directly from Spirit. It felt as if there were two distinct voices being spoken throughout the pages, my own personal voice and Spirit's universal voice. Those sections of the text where I felt that universal voice coming through have been indicated with the use of *italics*. I hope that you will be able to hear, through my voice and heart, the sound of Spirit's love for you. I hope that this love will open your heart to all that you already are.

My Choice of Words

As I wrote this book I struggled with the issue of which words to use to describe the numinous force of love that I experience. No one word or term can encompass and express what is essentially indescribable and ineffable, but I decided to use the words Spirit or Great Spirit, for the most part, but sometimes also the terms God/ Goddess, and "the divine" to represent what I feel. These terms resonate with me at a heart level. I'm aware that the use of the word God has fallen out of favor with many in recent years, for a variety of reasons. But I love what Dr. Martin Luther King, Jr. said on the subject: "You see, as long as love is around, God is alive. As long as justice is around, God is alive. There are certain conceptions of God that needed to die, but not God."[2]

Things That Matter

In a few chapters of this book I speak about what I perceive to be unpleasant truths about our culture and our world. While some may subscribe to the myth that if you're spiritual you shouldn't focus on what is negative or dark in the world and in yourself, I disagree. We need to be aware of what exists in order to heal it. How can we heal the wounds caused by racial and social inequality, by religious bigotry and persecution, and by materialism and militarism if we don't pay attention to them?

Deep down many of us do comprehend what is deeply out of balance in our inner and outer worlds, but we choose to look away and deny it because we're afraid of feeling uncomfortable and insecure. We're afraid of feeling adrift and helpless without the security of the illusions and beliefs we've bought into. But we can no longer afford to look away and allow the powers that have controlled us for so long to defile and destroy our natural world, including us.

I take support from great souls like Dr. King who discussed the danger of romanticizing the concept of a well-adjusted life in which we ignore the injustices of the world. In his book, *Strength to Love*, Dr. King stated that, "Human salvation lies in the hands of the creatively maladjusted,"[3] and, "In these days of worldwide confusion, there is a dire need for men and women who will courageously do battle for truth."[4] The great writer and spiritual philosopher, Jiddu Krishnamurti, has also been quoted as saying, "It is no measure of health to be well adjusted to a profoundly sick society." They both spoke of the need for a spiritual transformation within ourselves in order to have the strength to pursue what is ethical with a sense of humility and love, instead of with hatred and fear. In the vein of the movement called Sacred Activism, Krishnamurti urged us to begin the process of healing the world with self-knowledge, which will lead us to peace. "But to have peace, we will have to love, we will have to begin, not to live an ideal life, but to see things as they are and act upon them, transform them."[5]

Bibliography

There is an annotated bibliography at the end of this book in which I describe the amazing works that are mentioned throughout.

CHAPTER I

I Bless Every Moment

One day the sun admitted,

I am just a shadow …

I wish I could show you
When you are lonely or in darkness
The Astonishing Light
Of your own Being!

Hafiz[1]

My Early Years

I had been a depressed and troubled child, and I will share some of my childhood history, a history that I've come to see as my "story." It's a story about how I came to be so troubled, at least in part, even though I'm not defined by my past any more than you are defined by yours. We are not our stories. We are much, much more than our stories, our histories, or the sum of our experiences.

I emerged from my childhood with post-traumatic stress disorder, replete with recurring nightmares, occasional flashbacks (memories that suddenly come into consciousness in the form of a snapshot or an unfolding scene from a movie), and a persistent sense of needing to be alert and on guard. The trauma had begun when I was born. I believe that my mother lived with chronic, low level depression that became acute at times of high stress. She went into a severe, post-partum depression at my birth, as she had six years earlier when my sister, Joan, was born.

She'd had so little support from her family and friends when I was born that she felt despair going home from the hospital in the backseat of a taxi. No one, including my father, had come to accompany her and her newborn baby home—a baby she hadn't wanted in the first place. She felt completely ill-equipped, physically and emotionally, to care for another child. To add to her despair, my father, overwhelmed by his ever growing responsibilities, left home for a few weeks as he had when my sister was born. In her anguish she had even wanted to push my baby carriage with me in it off the roof of our Manhattan apartment building, but she fought the impulse with all of her strength. She told me these things when I was an adult, but babies are tuned in to the feelings of those around them, and I believe I understood that I was not a wanted child. In my infant's mind I interpreted her sorrow as a wish that I didn't exist.

My mother felt so alone and desperate after my birth that she was unable to even hold me, and after two or three days she felt compelled to give me to a couple she hardly knew who lived in our building. Even though I was too young to be able to put anything into words, on an emotional level I understood that I was being separated from my mother. I believe that I knew I had been *given away* and rejected since neither she nor I knew how long we'd be apart. The separation lasted only about a month and ended not because my mother was now capable of caring for me and wanted me back but because my father's sister stopped paying for my care. Although the physical separation had been brief it had done lasting psychological damage. This was just the first of many events in my childhood and adolescence that contributed to my sense that I was alone in the world and that this world was not to be trusted.

My earliest childhood memory, from about the age of two, relates to maternal separation as well. I remember looking up from the floor of the living room of my parents' home and watching my mother pick up her suitcase as she prepared to leave. She looked at me sadly and then walked out the front door. I was being abandoned again. I didn't cry, though. I just sat there. I think an emotional part of me had already shut down in the misguided attempt to avoid further pain. Years later I was told that she'd gone to the hospital for surgery and she wasn't sure she'd survive.

Adding to the distress and trauma of being physically without a loving maternal presence during my first month of life (and without one emotionally for many years after that), I was molested by the husband of the couple who took me in. This was revealed to me as an adult in a memory that bubbled up into consciousness while I was meditating with a good friend. She had mentioned wanting to heal a troublesome, life-long symptom and was wondering about its origin. She asked if I would give her the suggestion to allow her mind to go back to the time to when the symptom first appeared.

3

As I tuned in to what she was experiencing, an image soon formed in my mind of a man holding a newborn baby in distress. At first I assumed that the baby was my friend but something didn't feel right. This was not a dark haired, dark-eyed infant as my friend had been, but a blonde and blue-eyed one.

A shiver of electricity went through my body as I suddenly recognized myself as the baby. The man was touching me inappropriately and smirking. I wept with shock and sadness over the painful memory, as I did with many of the flashbacks. Even though the visions of what happened to me as an infant and a child were painful, I understood that they were re-experienced so that I could better understand what I'd been through and could then heal what needed to be healed.

A couple of weeks later, without divulging what he'd been doing, I described the man's appearance to my mother and asked her if she knew anyone like this who might have been around me as a baby. She said that I was describing the husband of the couple she'd given me to. She didn't ask why I was inquiring and I didn't offer the information. At that point in my life I wanted to spare her any further pain over what had happened in those years.

That man was the first of four men who would violate me by touching and fondling me by the time I was ten years old. The other three men were my father, who I believe had been sexually abused himself as a child, a friend's father who groped my developing breasts during two sleepovers at her house when I was nine or ten, and a stranger. The episode with the stranger happened when I was seven. I'd begged my mother to let me walk the three quarters of a mile into the neighboring town by myself to buy some moccasins. She finally relented and while I was alone with the shoe salesman, he touched me repeatedly. Then he sold me the moccasins. I didn't tell my mother what had happened, nor did I ever wear the moccasins.

Actually there was probably a fifth man who molested me when I was little. As I wrote this chapter, my PTSD got triggered from watching a documentary series about a pedophile priest and his friends and the cover-up of their crimes. I started having nightmares about being sexually attacked by the man who painted our house when I was a child. The dreams were terrifying and I sometimes woke myself up screaming for help. During that same time I also had a flash of a picture of him standing naked in front of me. That image appeared in my mind while I was meditating. My only conscious memory of him, though, is of his looking at me through the bathroom window as I took a bath and sang the theme song from the television series, "Davy Crockett." He would call me Davy Crockett and try to be friendly, but he never smiled and I never felt comfortable around him.

At the same time, a conscious memory I've had since childhood came to the fore. Interestingly, I'd never even tried to process it or understand it. The memory is of being a child of maybe five or six, alone in my parents' living room. A woman doctor comes into the room and asks me to lie down on the couch. She examines my genital area and then looks at me with alarm and sympathy. She says nothing, unfortunately, and walks out of the house. I'm left feeling scared and ashamed, and I wonder what I've done. I can only imagine that my parents called her because they saw the painter doing something to me. My sister remembers the painter's departure as being abrupt.

It amazes me how the conscious memory of an experience can be in one's mind but simultaneously be compartmentalized or closed off in terms of its meaning. Apparently this memory of the doctor examining me had been noted but sealed off from the rest of my mind, and not until I watched the courageous women on the documentary speak about retrieving and making sense of their memories, did I allow myself to realize the context and the meaning of the memory. The nightmares were just a signal from my deeper self asking me to pay attention to what was surfacing. They stopped as soon as I understood their import.

As a child I never told anyone about the two incidents of molestation that I had conscious awareness of. I'm not sure why, except that I have no memory of ever being told that I had the right to say No to any adult. I just felt as if being violated was the norm; it was what happened to children. Besides not being aware of my right to protect my personal space, I was a small child for my age and I was introverted and shy. I was an easy target. And not surprisingly, I would completely freeze when I was being violated, feeling utterly helpless. Even as a young adult, when male strangers took liberties with me, I would become immobilized. Actually, I can still freeze up when I feel hurt or threatened, but at least now I can be aware of my reaction in the moment when it occurs. I can then remind myself that I'm no longer a powerless, victimized child and I can choose to speak and act accordingly.

After adolescence it was rare for me to have spontaneous flashbacks of the past. In my mid-thirties, however, after having meditated almost daily for five years, I began to have occasional memories of my childhood come into my awareness again, like that memory of myself as a newborn. They usually occurred unprompted in the middle of deep and peaceful meditations. Another of those adult flashbacks was of my father molesting me as a very small child. It was a snapshot of him touching me in a sexual way and I have a look of sadness on my face. That picture put a lot of things in perspective and explained so many of the feelings I'd had about my father throughout my life.

My father was never able to honor my physical boundaries. For as long as I can remember I never ever wanted to be touched by him, even though I loved him dearly and longed for his approval.

Throughout my early childhood, until about age seven, he would often tell me to get into bed with him while he read his newspaper or news magazine. Believing that I had no choice I would comply, lying next to him and trying to be absolutely still. I don't remember him touching me in that situation but I was terrified that he would. For years I believed that my sister had managed to escape this situation, but I learned years later that the same thing had happened to her. As in my case, my mother looked on helplessly.

When I was 15, my father told me, in front of my mother, to join him in bed. By then I had the strength to say no, but my mother said nothing. She threw a pillow at me instead. I never asked her why she did that but I don't believe it was because I had rejected my father's offer. My feeling was that she resented the attention he was paying me that should have been going to her. And well into my twenties my father would try to kiss my neck, something that brought up rage and disgust in me. Most of the rage and shame and sense of powerlessness engendered by all of this I turned in on myself, amassing more and more self-hatred as the years passed.

There were many years growing up when my father worked evenings. His work was demanding and stressful and he found it necessary to have a few drinks after work before taking the train to our new home in the suburbs. He would be noticeably impaired, but when the work was especially stressful he would combine Phenobarbital with the alcohol. On those nights he would arrive home very drunk. There were many years in my adolescence when I would be afraid to go to sleep before he went to sleep, even if he didn't arrive home before one in the morning. I didn't want to be taken off guard. I didn't want to be startled awake by his sitting on my bed leaning over me, touching my arm or face. Those nights when he did come into my room and sit down I wanted to scream but I couldn't. I would just be gripped by fear of his touch. It never felt like the touch of a loving father.

There was physical mistreatment as well. As a small child I was hit sometimes by both parents and by a part-time housekeeper who helped out while my mother was incapacitated with depression. Another flashback memory I had in my thirties was of my father throwing me into my crib from a few feet away when I was about a year old. I hit my head on the headboard and was stunned, but quickly got up. Crying, I stood on my toes as I leaned against the railing of the crib for support and held my arms out to my father, entreating him to comfort me. He didn't. He just stood there and looked at me with contempt. I've replayed that scenario in emotional terms with men I've loved many times since then. I believe that I was still trying to elicit love from my father through men who reminded me of him on some level. It's a strategy that's destined to fail.

The worst of it, though, were the many years of emotional abuse from my father, who, no matter what he did to me and how much anger I may have had toward him, was still my beloved "Daddy." His shaming of me, his ridicule of my spirit, his raging and sarcasm, coming out of nowhere to a child's understanding, created a great deal of confusion and grief in me and added to my self-loathing. For example, when I was nine, he ridiculed me for being delighted that my body had started to change and develop. He expressed contempt for the pride I felt about my growing breasts and would say things to my mother in front of me to shame me. I don't know what demons he was trying to keep at bay then, but he started calling me a whore when I was thirteen even though I was a virgin until I was eighteen. Given my history with both parents, from that point on I was ashamed of my body and of my sexuality and sometimes even of my very existence. The stage was set for me to wage war against my body and myself.

Part of being at war with my body was an ongoing battle with food. I regarded food at once as both my solace and my enemy. Starting in early adolescence I became a compulsive overeater. I believe I was trying to dull the pain that was such a part of my daily life. I was trying to numb the grief and rage not only over my father's actions but also over my mother's inaction, her emotional abandonment of me. That unsuccessful attempt to use food to suppress or not feel my feelings lasted for several years. Then, as often happens, for a few years in my twenties I was anorexic, literally starving myself. At the most severe point of the disorder I was skeletal, my weight an alarming 87 pounds. People who hadn't seen me for a while would gasp when they first saw me at that weight, but I simply couldn't understand what the problem was. I wonder now if starving myself was a semi-conscious attempt to kill myself, since I battled a suicidal impulse on a regular basis for many years. When I look back on my early life there are times I wonder how I was able to stay alive. But I did manage to stay alive, even though it took many years and a lot of strength to even begin to face the wounds that my father inflicted—and that my mother ignored—and heal them.

The combined effects of the abandonment by my mother and the emotional and sexual abuse by my father and other men had completely compromised my sense of self. I now understand that when there is early and significant separation from one's mother, the feeling of having been rejected and abandoned can create deep psychological wounds in a child. In the mind of the little girl and later the adolescent that I was then, my sense of having worth, my sense of even being worthy of love, was painfully in doubt.

In large part, I believe that whatever perceived value I had had become unconsciously equated with being sexually attractive to men. Of course the larger culture contributes to this as well, with the sexualization of ever younger children by the entertainment and apparel industries. Girls, especially, are subtly and not so subtly encouraged to see their worth only as sexual objects for adults. So for many years I was stuck in the mindset of believing that sexual attention was love. It's not, and it's certainly not a foundation on which to develop a sense of being someone of value in the world. Quite the contrary. For many years of my life I believed that I had no intrinsic value at all.

As *so many* of us now know, being sexually objectified and then violated as an infant or a child, female or male, steals something from the soul. It steals our sense of being able to trust that the world around us is a safe place in which to thrive or even to exist. It can steal our sense of knowing our inherent worth as a human being. And because we are too young to have the words or the conceptual framework within which to understand what is happening, we often unconsciously take on the guilt and shame of the violator. To our child's mind, if this powerful and beloved person is abusing us then there must be something bad about us, not them. Or perhaps when we're little, any authority figure, be it a parent or teacher or clergy person, has a kind of moral imperative over us and can elicit a latent sense of shame and guilt that has already been acculturated into us.

It's often said that the abuse steals our innocence as well. While I understand what people mean by that statement, I suggest that there is nothing—no experience, no event, no behavior—that can take away the original innocence and purity that you and I were born with, even if that innocence gets covered over with layers of conditioning and forgetfulness. Ultimately, though, some part of our spirit can *seem* to die, and some of us are never able to bring that part back to life.

What I say now to the small, self-hating child I was then, and also perhaps to your inner child, "Listen, angel, it's not. your. fault. The people who are entrusted to take care of you don't know any better. They're not conscious. And deep down they really hate *themselves*. Perhaps they're reliving and recreating what was done to them as a child. They didn't deserve what was done to them any more than you deserve what is being done to you. It's not your fault, angel. I love you."

My Parents' Pain

My mother's own childhood had been marred by her mother's emotional abuse which tore her down at every turn. Adding to her sense of inferiority, her mother forced her to leave high school just before graduating to take care of a sibling. She never really got over the loss and the blow to her self-esteem. When our mother was 90, however, my sister, now Dr. Joan Rossi, Ed.D., contacted the head of Mom's old school district in upstate New York. He awarded Mom an earned high school diploma, with the one missing credit being made up for by life experience. Holding the diploma in her hands, she wept and declared, "Now I am someone." It was heart-breaking to realize that she had secretly defined her worth through an outward accomplishment, even though she never defined anyone else in that way. She did understand—when it came to *others*—that the essential worth of any human life is so much more than academic or work-related achievement can measure. My sister and I were thrilled to help her celebrate her new diploma and all that it meant to her, as we reminded her of all that she had accomplished without her diploma, like all the years of selfless volunteer work and all of the love she'd given to her family and her world.

For much of her life our mother never really knew her own worth. Consequently she was never able to develop the self-confidence to navigate the world well enough to know how to get her needs met. Nor did she have a solid spiritual foundation that would have given her an ongoing resource that she could have drawn strength from. When she was suffering from full-blown depression, the only way she could cope with her pain was by withdrawing from her life, at least in the years when my sister and I were little. This left some major deficits in her parenting abilities. Essentially she was not able to really be there for us, physically or emotionally, which included not protecting us from our father's dark side. She didn't have the skills, nor the self-esteem and courage needed to have used those skills, to even protect herself. Regardless of my mother's abdication of many of her maternal responsibilities, I'm grateful that she did not physically abandon us by committing suicide. She had to have had great strength to persevere, essentially unsupported, through years of deep clinical depression.

She also suffered from terrible anxiety, and in those years even traditional medicine provided almost no treatment options to ease the pain of anxiety or depression. For a few years her anxiety was focused in a fear of leaving the house. But with little kindness or support from her world, she knew that if she wanted to heal she would have to face her fears by herself and do what needed to be done in spite of them. Again as a testament to her strength of will and her determination, one day she forced herself to leave the house—alone—and walk the quarter mile or so to the nearby shopping area. She bought what she needed and walked back home. With one splendid act of bravery she had begun to heal.

When all is said and done my mother was a lovely and gentle woman who was remarkably without guile. And though she would not have won an award for her parenting skills, she preserved even the outward appearance of her original innocence throughout her life. She was kind and funny and smarter than some people gave her credit for, and I am so grateful that she was my mother.

My father struggled to keep his emotional head above water most of the time. He didn't talk a lot about his childhood except in idealized ways, but there had to have been a lot of trauma since he lived with an alcoholic father, a younger brother diagnosed with schizophrenia at age sixteen, and a mother who attempted suicide twice. For as long as I can remember he was a deeply unhappy and unfulfilled man. He told us more than once that he believed he was a failure because he had never made a lot of money and had published only one book. We knew him as a gifted print and broadcast journalist and fiction writer, but in his mind, his accomplishments were not sufficient criteria for success or happiness. Neither was the fact that he had a loving family, all of whom would've done almost anything to help him to be happy. We felt sad that we meant so little to his sense of well-being and that he had bought into the myth that public recognition and material wealth were the only measures of a life's meaning. Of course, there may have been other things that contributed to his sense of failure in life, like shame and guilt, but he didn't speak about those things. A few weeks before he died, however, he did tell my mother that he was burdened with a lot of guilt. She didn't ask him why.

At heart my father was a decent and talented man and he was often ahead of his time. He cared deeply about social justice, as did my mother, and he championed and wrote about the concept of social security for workers years before it was introduced as government policy. And both my parents knew that all people deserved respect regardless of superficial differences like skin color or religion. My father loved to recount the story of riding a bus with my pregnant mother years ago somewhere in the South and giving his seat to an elderly African American woman. The bus driver stopped the bus and demanded that my father take his seat back. He refused and he and my mother were forced to leave the bus.

When I reflect on my father's life now, I can only offer him empathy and deep gratitude. He may have wanted to die sometimes, as he told me, but he never took his own life. He may have wanted to go off somewhere and live alone and do nothing but write, as he once told us, but he never abandoned his family. He supported us as best he could year after year, which was no small feat considering what a deeply wounded soul he was. He showed up, as they say, and he did his best to live and love. And a few weeks before he died he gave me a great gift of love. He told me that I had the most beautiful heart of anyone he'd ever known. I was dumbfounded and all I could do was cry.

I took care of my mother for the last several years of her life, and we became closer during that time. Since I had done a good deal of my own healing by that time and had made peace with most of the issues I'd had with my parents, I was able to help her to do some emotional healing as well. She was able to forgive her mother and my father for their having hurt her, and more importantly, she was able to forgive herself. I told her that I only wanted her to be happy and that she could give me the gift of releasing the past. During her last few years she did find the strength (and it does take strength) to let go of the guilt that she had carried for decades. At the end of her life she was lighthearted and peaceful. She died at home at the age of 93. Unfortunately I did not have the same opportunity to help my father, who had died suddenly at the age of 77.

Getting Stuck in Our Stories

Unfortunately some of us get stuck at the story level of our lives. We forget who we truly are and who we can be *now*, regardless of what has happened to us or what we have done. We can get stuck in the pattern of interpreting everything in our lives only from the perspective of our childhood and adolescent traumas. We can get caught in the feeling and the belief that we are still powerless victims, much as we may have felt when we were little. In a way we live out a kind of life script that was written for us years ago by those around us and by our own unconscious mind.

In his masterful book, *Toward a Psychology of Awakening: Buddhism,*

Psychotherapy, and the Path of Personal and Spiritual Transformation, transpersonal psychologist, John Welwood, has written about how, as defenseless children, we contract around overwhelming, painful feelings, and how we can build our whole identity around the avoidance of those painful experiences. We then create "an elaborate web of rationalizations—'stories' about the way we are or the way reality is—to justify our denial and avoidance."[2] Our stories are almost never conscious, however, which makes it difficult to let them go.

I have read that when we're stalled at the stage of living out our stories we run the risk of "wearing our wounds," which is to say we're always at the ready to see ourselves being wounded again and again in the course of our daily interactions with others. We may actually be drawing the wounding experiences to ourselves by our combative energy or we may be perceiving insults and hurt where there are none. If we want to heal, though, there will come a time when we realize that we need to let go of defining and imagining ourselves in ways that are based solely on our past experiences. At some point we need to release the narrative thread of our history and risk just being here and now. We have to take the chance to be open to life as it is right now, not as it was years ago. And we need to be willing to open to ourselves just as we are right now, sensitive and vulnerable, not as who we felt we needed to be in the past.

On the other hand, there is value in reflecting on the story line of our lives. Our histories can help us understand how we've gotten to where we are, what has motivated our behavior, and how we've created the lives we're now living. That understanding can help us to have *compassion for ourselves*—for our having carried around the old hurts and resentments for so long. In that regard I remember watching a video once in which a woman was describing what it felt like to be on the "other side of the veil" during a near-death experience. She recounted the process of doing a review of her life from childhood and how that gave her insight into how her behavior had been shaped by her early experiences. I believe she said something like, "So that's why I've felt that way my whole life."

For those of us who have not had the opportunity to do an early-life review during a near-death event, maybe we can give ourselves the benefit of the doubt in the meantime and have a little loving kindness for ourselves. Most likely there were many influences and events in our infancy and childhood that shaped our attitudes and behavior and that may still be affecting us. I know that compassion is not always valued in our world since it is considered by some to represent weakness. But compassion, for ourselves and others, is the first step in healing—in remembering and embracing the innocent and perhaps wounded inner child who is still alive within us. Additionally, understanding our stories and sharing them may give hope and encouragement and guidance to others who are going through similar experiences.

Taking Responsibility for My Healing

For many years I struggled with what seemed like a boundless font of anger toward both of my parents, allowing the anger to mask deep feelings of grief. It was easier to feel self-righteous anger than it was to experience the pain of betrayal by those who were entrusted with my care. After my father's death, however, it became easier to release a lot of the anger since my mother and sister and I were finally able to admit what we'd all known for a long time but had been afraid to say out loud: that he'd been an alcoholic as had his father before him. It was a relief to finally be able to have some kind of conceptual framework within which to make some sense of the family history.

After reading about the patterns of unconscious family dynamics that are often present in families with an alcoholic parent, we began to have some insight into his behavior and our own. We realized that my mother fit the classic role of the Enabler, and I, as second born child, fit the role of Scapegoat for the family. My sister, as first born, had been a classic example of the Hero child. So many experiences and incidents were now understandable from this new perspective, a compassionate perspective that blamed no one and helped us to understand the disease of alcoholism.

As the years went on I did my best to heal the sadness that had permeated my life. The healing began with having to acknowledge that I had taken on my family's version of me as their black sheep. That acknowledgment gave me the impetus to discover what I was really feeling and to honor that. I came to realize that I wasn't crazy for feeling what I had felt for so long, but the childhood defense of hardening to my feelings had kept me out of my own heart. I knew I had to find a way back in, and I committed to the ongoing journey.

As I healed, I had to unearth and relinquish old, limiting self-images and worn out, restrictive ways of viewing the possibilities of life, and I knew I had to release my sense of being a victim. It was a gradual process, but I remember coming to the realization that if I were a victim of my parents' behavior as well as the influences of a toxic society, so then were my parents victimized by their parents and their world. As I was able to see my parents through the lens of a long line of previous generations of parents, all wounded by their families and by their unbalanced cultures, it was easier to come to them without judgment and recrimination.

Most importantly, perhaps, I came to appreciate that whatever harm was done to me as a child, by my parents or anyone else, it was now *my* responsibility to heal. Not only is it our own responsibility as adults to heal our childhood wounds, it isn't even *possible* for anyone else to heal them. Even if one has parents who have the courage to take an honest look at themselves and admit any harm they may have done, they cannot magically erase all the consequences of what was done. Nor can they do the adult child's emotional work of recognizing and feeling their own feelings and then moving through them. On the other hand, if a parent can risk feeling deeply vulnerable and ask for forgiveness from a child, it's an incredible gift to give. It's a gift that validates and honors the child's experience, a gift that says You're not crazy or sick and you didn't deserve this. But whether or not we receive this gift from a parent, the truth remains that only we can free ourselves from our suffering.

I Bless Every Moment

This may be hard to believe but I have come to bless every moment of my difficult childhood and adolescence because, ultimately, the experiences I went through helped me to deepen my very capacity to feel compassion for others. Somehow the years of painful experiences ultimately allowed me to *open*—to open up to everything—instead of shutting me down. The words of an old Carly Simon song come to mind in relation to this, "Don't mind if I fall apart, there's more room in a broken heart." I like to think of it as a broken *open* heart. I'm also reminded of a story I read several years ago about an art museum's exhibit of a so-called disabled artist's work. It was described in an extraordinary book entitled, *Heal Thy Self: Lessons on Mindfulness in Medicine* by Dr. Saki Santorelli. (The story may be apocryphal since I haven't been able to identify the sculptor, but it's stunning nonetheless.) The exhibit contained a piece of sculpture that consisted of a large ball of polished stone that had been smashed into pieces and then put back together, the pieces held in place by bolts and bonding agents. The piece was called "Shattered but Still Whole."

I mentioned what I remembered of that sculpture several years later when I had the joy of attending a day's workshop called "Writing from the Heart," given by the extraordinary writer and teacher, Nancy Aronie. One of the day's exercises was to write for just 15 minutes on the topic, "What I didn't tell you then …" This is what I wrote:

> What I didn't tell you then … is that my heart breaks for you, Dad, for the torment you must have felt when you demeaned me repeatedly and molested me and made me feel ashamed for your behavior. But you died too soon, way before I'd healed enough to be able to come to you, heart to heart, one human soul to another. I didn't know enough then about the depth of the pain you had to have felt to treat your sweet and beautiful baby girl like an object of your derision (although your later threats of suicide gave me a clue).
>
> I couldn't tell you then that it's really okay—you didn't break me. I'm reminded of that piece of sculpture I read about once—a ball of concrete broken into many pieces and then put back together, the pieces held in place with unifying wire. The piece was called Shattered but Still Whole. I was shattered by my childhood but I'm still whole, Dad. I'm still innocent and full of God's light.
>
> And I can tell you now that the childhood you and Mom created for me was truly a "poorly wrapped gift." Those experiences deepened my capacity to feel compassion for the suffering of all beings. Now I can help those who feel unlovable because I've been there. I know how that feels, and I know it's not the truth.

As a direct result of what I went through I know that there is no experience, no pain that a child or an adult can go through that I can't empathize with or identify with and wish to relieve. My own pain has helped me to know, deep down to my bones, that I am connected to the feelings—the joy and the pain—of all beings. It is not just *my* joy or *my* fear or *my* sense of triumph, it is *ours*.

All of the hardships of my early years also taught me to be extremely sensitive to others' feelings. I was conditioned as a child to be exquisitely tuned in to the feelings and moods of my parents and the other adults around me in order to ascertain what they needed and what I could do that would protect me from their harm. This quality of vigilance, however, which was born of fear, has ultimately served me well in my work and in my life through the development of my intuition. From having carefully studied those around me for clues about their state of mind, I learned to detect subtle changes in facial expressions and gestures. On a deeper level I was learning to attune myself to people's *energy*. I think we all come into the world being able to feel the energy of those around us but we forget this capability since it is not usually acknowledged or encouraged by the world we're born into. Everything that I went through also gave me the opportunity to bring an end to the family history of child abuse. It has stopped with my sister and me.

Lastly, I bless the painful experiences of my early years because they've helped me in my life's work of helping people to feel loved. I can say with authority that I know what it feels like to believe that you are unworthy of love. I know what it feels like to wonder if the earth would be better off without you. I know the grief that underlies those feelings. I have been there and I know now that it is not the truth. It's not the truth for a single one of us, whoever we appear to be. I know now that we are all dearly loved.

Spirit is whispering to you now ...

Dream with me now, Beloved, until you remember that you are worthy of love, whoever you are in the eyes of the world. Dream with me now as you remember that you are known and honored and so dearly loved by this Great Spirit who dreams joyful worlds of living light into form eon after eon. Remember with me that underneath the layers of forgetfulness, your glorious heart remains pure, and your innate goodness is shining through your tears.

I know your heart, Dear One, because it is my heart. And I am blessing you now and embracing you with a love so profound and so bright that it fills every cell and consciousness of your being with bliss. Can you imagine it, Dear One? Can you allow it to be real?

*Can you imagine that beneath the surface appearance of all of your life – that you are the light of my love on earth? You **are** this love, at heart, as are all beings, and it is all the spiritual knowing you will ever really need.*

CHAPTER II

Coming to the Truth of Love Your Own Way

... something ignited in my soul, fever or unremembered wings,
and I went my own way,
deciphering that burning fire,
and I wrote the first bare line,
bare, without substance, pure
foolishness,
pure wisdom
of one who knows nothing,
and suddenly I saw
the heavens
unfastened
and open.

Pablo Neruda[1]

The Gift of Bach

I offer you the amazing possibility that, in our deepest selves, you and I already have access to the Source of everything—everything we'll ever really need to be awake and fulfilled in this life! The problem is that most of us forget that we know this. In fact, it would be difficult to find a person, no matter how evolved, who has never felt disconnected from this Source and from their own deepest truth. So how do we begin to access and remember this knowing? We begin to remember by quieting our minds and our lives through conscious intention, through mindfulness and meditation, and then by learning to trust what we experience and *feel* to be right for *us*.

My own journey of remembering began years ago. Disillusioned with Catholicism (and with life in general), I had dropped out of my church at age 16. By that time, I was wary of anything related to what others referred to as God, and I even doubted the existence of any kind of higher power. I was questioning everything, including the dogma and the assumptions on which my religion was based— or should I say my experience of that religion. The church that my family attended was not a warm and welcoming place. There seemed to be little sense of spiritual community among the congregants, unless you were among the families who sent their children to the church-affiliated school. My sister and I attended weekly catechism class for years where we were required to memorize the tenets and rules of the religion. There was no talk of love that I can remember and questions were not encouraged. My most salient memory from those classes was the terror I felt at age ten when the nun told me that if I didn't return the confirmation robe the following week she would "skin me alive."

The only love I knew at that church was the love that I shared in my teenage years with the cats who lived around the church. (I'm madly in love with animals.) They would follow me up the stone steps of the church to be petted and loved. On one occasion a cat who was not happy that I had left her to go inside meowed so loudly and plaintively at the side door of the church that she started to disturb the parishioners, although some did smile. I had to slip outside to quiet her down and I happily remained with her until the service was over.

There was one other time that I have a clear memory of feeling love within our church. I was maybe three or four years old and a visiting bishop was speaking to the congregation. He didn't stand at the podium looking down at us to speak but sat on the lower level of the altar, with the railing to the altar opened. I was so drawn to his gentle manner that I went to sit at his feet and suck my thumb while I held his soft robe to my cheek. (My memory is that his robe was dark red velvet but that may be wrong.) My father tried to call me back but the bishop smiled and waved his hand to indicate that it was okay. It was a little bit of heaven. When all was said and done, however, after many years in that congregation, all I knew was that my church's encouragement of fear and guilt did not resonate within me as the truth.

For many years, I had to say "No" to whatever was *not* my truth while I searched for what that truth was. I sampled the knowledge and experience of different spiritual philosophies and practices— reading books, attending services, and taking seminars. Each path or practice offered something meaningful and lovely but taken as a whole, each proved somehow unsatisfactory. Not a lot of what I sampled resonated as heart-felt truth for me. Eventually, as I said "No" over and over again, I began to wonder if something was lacking in me. Maybe I didn't have the intellectual or emotional capacity to recognize what was so compelling in these traditions and their rituals. But it turned out that there was nothing lacking in me or in the different paths that I tried; it was just that none of them was right for me at that time. In that regard I also believe that my natural wariness of groups and group-think was a hint from my soul that I wasn't supposed to take on anyone else's belief system.

Looking back now, I know that a state of uncertainty was the best state I could have been in (and usually still is) because it allowed me to open to a new perspective. Without words to describe it then, I had the Beginner's Mind, where the possibilities are endless and no beliefs are set in stone. (I love what Vincent van Gogh wrote to his brother Theo, "For my part I know nothing with any certainty, but the sight of the stars makes me dream."[2]) By the time I was a young adult, my uncertainty, my *not knowing* had allowed for an opening to the reality of my own feelings and my own experience to occur. That opening allowed Spirit in—to energetically burst me wide open.

Back then I was in a Ph.D. program at a university in New York. The school was near a botanical garden, and in my spare time I used to love to walk and jog through the woods there. One late August day at the beginning of my second year of the program, I felt that something was amiss as I walked along a familiar path. My ankle had started to hurt and when I looked down I saw that it was swollen and had a bluish tinge to it. After a few days I began to feel like I had the flu, with fever, a painful and stiff neck, and terrible fatigue. I thought it would pass but it didn't. I went to several physicians but none could tell me what I had, although one well-known rheumatologist did say I had some sort of arthritic process in my joints (but didn't suggest further tests or a treatment plan). Mostly they just suggested that I consult a psychiatrist.

As the months went on I slid into the darkness of severe, chronic illness. I was suffering with debilitating muscle pain, swollen and painful joints, weight loss, hair loss, and profound depression. Forced to relinquish a fellowship at the university, I still couldn't give anyone a definitive diagnosis to explain or justify what I and my supervisors perceived to be my failure. This just increased the trauma of the illness.

Being so sick, I would stay with my mother for extended periods of time so she could help take care of me. Adding to the mix, my friends had withdrawn from me, perhaps partly out of weariness with my depression and partly out of fear that what I was experiencing could happen to them. My much-loved boyfriend had also left me in search of someone "normal." I was bereft over losing him and I cried for months afterward. As he left, though, he did suggest that I learn to meditate, even though he did not do so himself. He told me that it might give me some peace. I filed his suggestion away in my mind—to be retrieved at a later time.

During that same time my family and I were devastated by the sudden death of my father from a heart attack. It was a time of great grief for me, especially since I had unresolved issues with him. I didn't understand then how any of the old hurts could be resolved if he were no longer physically present and no longer able to respond. As I got older, though, I came to know that I could do all the resolving of anguished, unfinished business that I needed to by myself—by doing my best to deeply understand him and his own pain, forgiving him, and by understanding my lesson (and thus the inherent value) in all of it— within my own heart.

He did, however, give me a wonderful gift the night after he died. He came to me in a dream, appearing as a vibrant young man. He was sitting amidst a group of his friends who were milling about, lamenting his passing. He didn't say a word but gave me a knowing smile while telepathically telling me, "They think I'm no longer alive, but we know better, don't we?" I was so grateful for the experience since it was immensely comforting to have reassurance of his ongoing life after death, but still this weight of grief colored everything I experienced for a long time.

Not long after his death, my mother, who had converted to Catholicism in order to marry him forty years prior, decided to return to Presbyterianism, the religion in which she'd been raised. Once, when I was physically able, I accompanied her to church. Prolonged illness had taken its toll on my appearance, and I was a sight—virtually skin and bones with most of my hair gone. But we sat in this lovely little church in suburban New York, clutching each other's hand as we listened to music from the Skinner organ being played by a virtuoso. When he played anything by Bach or Widor's Toccata from Symphony No. 5, the stunning beauty of the sound so moved us that tears fell down our cheeks. The energy and vibration of the music touched something very deep inside, something hopeful and joyful in us, even though we barely dared to let ourselves feel hope or joy. While we couldn't put anything into words at the time, we just knew that this beauty was food for our hungry souls.

In an attempt to try to recreate those lovely feelings, I purchased recordings of the powerful music we had heard in church. One oppressively hot July afternoon, alone on the living room floor, I listened to Bach's Toccata and Fugue in D minor. Closing my eyes in an attempt to quiet my mind, I did my best to push the familiar feeling of despair out of my awareness, if only for a few moments. I also acknowledged a kind of half-hearted intention to find out the truth about the existence of any higher power.

Then it happened. All I can say is that the sheer joy and magic of the sound of Bach took my consciousness to a place it had never been before, a place that seemed to transcend this world. I felt what can only be described as an energetic tidal wave of feeling, a *force of pure love* pouring over me and through me. It was a kind of love that I had not experienced before in this life—truly without qualification or condition. I was loved regardless how many mistakes I'd made or what I'd done wrong or had failed to do. Not only did I feel that I was forgiven for anything I had ever done, it felt like there was nothing, really, that needed to be forgiven. I knew then that, ultimately, it is *we* who have to forgive *ourselves* when we forget about God.

I also had the distinct feeling that this love was so huge that my little body could not have physically handled the full force of this love, even if I had been 10 feet tall! It felt like my body was a wire that could only handle 1000 volts, while the full force of the love would be a million volts! Years later I read with delight these lines from Rumi, the celebrated Sufi mystic and poet from the thirteenth century: "I am so small I can barely be seen. How can this great love be inside me?"[3] I know exactly what he meant.

In that same moment I was given the awareness that my consciousness was connected to all other consciousness everywhere. In the flash of a moment I felt and understood that I was intimately connected to all beings and to all of life. I knew that I was loved because I existed, and I existed as a part of the whole of what I've now come to understand as the Universal Mind. The experience was beyond words, and the poignancy of feeling so loved when I was afraid I wasn't really lovable made me weep. Immediately I felt that this was the love of Spirit. This was divine love—what some people called God or Goddess, and I knew that this love was my very essence and the essence of everyone else in the world.

In what seemed like an instant, I could feel that I was a spark of the fire of divine love, and I had been changed forever. I'd had the *experience* of this love, and there was no way to erase it or negate it or forget it. It's as if one moment you're on one side of the Grand Canyon and the next moment you've crossed over to the other side. You don't know how you got there, and you know that there is no road back.

My own deep experience of transcendent, all-encompassing love was the beginning (and truly *just* the beginning) of my healing—on all levels. It was the beginning of healing my sense of being separate from the rest of the world and my secret, shameful sense of being unlovable that I had carried with me from childhood. Of course, this healing and becoming conscious is an ongoing, lifelong process, and it can only occur one mindful moment at a time.

Taking Off the Masks

In order for me to begin hear Spirit's voice, Spirit had helped me to remove many of the masks my ego had been wearing—all of the life roles I had played and with which I had overidentified. Spirit showed me that with the advent of unrelenting and debilitating illness I could no longer say I was a good student, a productive worker, an attractive woman, or a good daughter or friend or lover. These narrow roles within which I had defined myself were obliterated; it felt like they'd been ripped out from under me. Nothing of how I comfortably defined myself was left. There were no more masks to cling to and hide behind.

What did remain was a vulnerability, a "not knowing," and a hint of my intention to awaken. Spirit took it from there. Looking back, even though I was most often confused and terrified (of living, more than dying), I realize now that all I had to do was to open my mind and heart *a little bit,* and Spirit just rushed right in. As I continued to open to Spirit I believe that I experienced what Buddhism has called "bright faith." In her eloquent book, *Faith: Trusting Your Own Deepest Experience,* Buddhist teacher Sharon Salzberg describes bright faith as the "state of love-filled delight in possibilities and the eager joy of actualizing them."[4] This kind of faith can give us the energy and courage to leave behind our cynicism and what is familiar and safe as we explore the unknown. It's not to be confused with blind faith which is associated with an unquestioning devotion to a doctrine or a teacher. Ms. Salzberg suggests instead that we choose to have faith in our own awareness and understanding and in what our own deepest experiences reveal to us.

Rain from Heaven

Not long after the experience of being "broken open" while listening to that heavenly music, Spirit gave me the experience of its love once again. It gave me evidence again that I was known and loved no matter the outward appearance of my life or how desolate I felt. And desolate is the word. In addition to the swollen joints, muscle pain, and constant fatigue I was experiencing, the clinical depression I was going through deepened, and was now accompanied by severe and unrelenting anxiety that seemed to grip my mid-section. (It wasn't until 17 long years later that the symptoms would be diagnosed as Lyme disease.) I was hospitalized briefly for treatment of the depression and anxiety, but nothing helped. One of the less-than-therapeutic interventions by a psychiatric resident there was the stunning pronouncement that I needed to "completely redo my personality" in order to heal my depression. I had no idea what he meant nor the strength to question him about it. I just felt more overwhelmed and hopeless.

Once home, every day was a new struggle with gut-wrenching anxiety, physical pain, and unremitting, utter despair. I thought of suicide often although I didn't really want to die; I just wanted the pain of hopelessness to stop. Even though my recent shift of consciousness was always in the back of my mind, it still took all of my physical and emotional strength to continue to go to classes, to be able to study, and some days, to just stay alive. Somehow, though, I made a decision to live the best I could until I died, no matter when that might be, and I just kept going.

I kept going with "one day at a time" (sometimes it was even one breath at a time) as my mantra for more than a year. The course work for my degree was almost complete, and soon it would be time to begin my dissertation research. I didn't have a clue about which research topic to choose, and the question weighed on my mind. One quiet Sunday afternoon I decided to try to meditate for the purpose of receiving guidance from Spirit on selecting a focus for my research. I closed my eyes and attempted to relax and quiet my thoughts. Soon a kind of foggy mist appeared in my mind's eye, and I began to glimpse hazy images of words in the distance. The letters of the words seemed to be made of light. The first word to emerge out of the mist was "Rain." That didn't make any sense to me, but another word was forming and coming forward. It was "from"… and the last word was "Heaven." Rain from Heaven. What did *that* mean? I had no idea, but I knew that it was not a topic for a dissertation. I was puzzled but also a little annoyed that whoever or whatever was communicating with me had given me this seemingly silly message.

The next morning, while I was upstairs studying, I had the strange and sudden feeling of being guided to go downstairs. I didn't know why, but I went downstairs into the living room. The TV was on although no one was watching, and I found myself staring kind of blankly and absentmindedly at the program on the screen. It was the old game show called "Password." The game consisted of two opposing teams trying to guess the password; one member of each team provided a one-word clue and the other member made a guess. The team that guessed the correct word won the round.

I had only been standing there for a couple of moments when something got my attention. One member of the first team had just offered the clue "rain," and the other player guessed the word "showers." No, that was not correct. Over to the other team, where one member offered the clue "heaven" and his teammate shot back with the correct word, "manna." MANNA! Rain from Heaven is

MANNA! A chill went up my spine as I heard the word, and tears welled up in my eyes (I cried a lot in those years—actually, I still do, but it's often for joy). I stood there astonished for a minute or two, trying to take it all in.

I had heard the word manna from time to time in conversation, and I had the feeling it meant sustenance or grace from the other side of the veil. But I wanted a deeper understanding of the concept, so I looked up the details in my father's old bible reference book. In the story of Exodus 16, manna was the name the Israelites gave to the food that was miraculously supplied by God as they wandered through the wilderness for 40 years! It was a gift from God to sustain them. This message for me, delivered so dramatically, let me know that as I wandered through my own wilderness, I was not alone. It let me know that I was known and cherished by Spirit, and that I was being supplied with whatever I needed to make it through.

In the Exodus parable it was significant that this manna that appeared every morning could not be hoarded. If they tried to put aside the manna that they didn't eat in a day, out of fear that it might not appear again the next morning, it went bad. They had to face their fear of starvation and death and give over to trust, since acting out of fear accomplished the opposite of what they wanted. But throughout their time of wandering, the Israelites did come to trust that as surely as the sun would rise in the east every morning, manna would fall from heaven. It would fall as long as they needed it and it would be bountiful. They came to trust that heaven, the *Source,* would provide for them—one day at a time.

The message for all of us is that Spirit, the *Source,* loves us and is supporting us all the time. And since we are an integral part of Spirit, Spirit's resources are our resources. When we forget that truth and cling in fear to something that is meant to flow through in our lives, as in trying to hoard the manna overnight, we experience pain and we block the free flow of our energy. Decisions we make that are based solely on the fear of loss of some kind, like choosing to remain in a job or a relationship that no longer serves us, often result in regret. Fear may also motivate us to try to resist the experience of something, like avoiding situations or relationships that we think we can't handle. Isn't it interesting that frequently our fears are based on what we imagine *could* happen sometime in the future? We're afraid that we won't be able to cope with what hasn't yet occurred.

I'm not trying to minimize the effect that fear can have on us, though. I know it can be difficult to try again when we've felt nearly paralyzed by anxiety. Fear arises in me on a daily basis. Sometimes it's just a passing anxious thought that can be easily dismissed, but once in a while I can get caught in a veritable whirlpool of dread and self-doubt, forgetting that I am a spark of Spirit's love and that that love is my source. When I finally realize that I've been nurturing my fears again and have gotten stuck in them, I remind myself that I can take back my power. I do my best to see my fears as just messengers, bringing me the message of where ***I have (seemingly) separated myself from the love of Spirit***. I remind myself that everything that happens in my life is co-created with Spirit (and everyone else) out of a higher order love and for my higher good. Then (often but not always!) I can do what needs to be done in spite of my fear.

You and I are being challenged to remain in present moment awareness and do nothing less than dare to trust—trust in the love of Spirit for us and within us. We're being asked to dare to trust in our own experience and our own basic goodness even though this is sometimes easier said than done. All I can promise is that it does get easier to trust in life's process as we take the chance to test out the idea that this Source is really there for us. It gets easier to trust as we take that chance to test out the ***radical idea that life is on our side***. You and I are being asked to remember that throughout our lives, whenever we feel lost in some personal desert or whenever we feel caught in a web of fear, we are receiving and will continue to receive this rain from heaven, this "bread of the wilderness" from Spirit.

Ultimately, the guidance I received that Sunday was not the dissertation title I thought I needed. It was something much greater—unmistakable evidence that a conscious force of love was working on my behalf while I struggled through some dark years. Somehow this force of love, this Spirit, knew me and knew what I really needed. It was communicating to me that I would never be alone. It was helping me then to get through that anguished period of my life, and it is helping me still. This force of divine love that is the very breath of the universe knows *you* as well and is helping *you* now and always.

Honoring Your Own Experience

It is our right and our responsibility to allow our own experience to uncover what is real for us. It's not the right of the dominant culture to tell us what is valuable and real and what is not. Yet living in the modern world, we are besieged with a constant barrage of overt and subliminal messages that reinforce certain societal standards and norms in all media, including television, films, video games, popular music, etc. These messages are presented through advertising as well as program content, and they continually strengthen—and *create*—the prevailing value system of the dominant culture. Many of these values contain elements of relentless violence and militarism, racism and misogyny, cut-throat competition, and the exploitation and destruction of the natural environment. These are not my values and they may not be yours.

In their deeply thoughtful book, *Healing the Future: Personal Recovery from Societal Wounding*, authors Dennis Linn, Sheila Fabricant Linn and Matthew Linn elucidate just how these kinds of societal factors can impact us in significantly negative ways. They suggest that throughout our lives, not only do we carry familial and interpersonal woundedness with us from childhood, we also carry the woundedness from a toxic and often degenerate social and cultural environment. This toxicity can "color our energy, color our existence and drive us into a trancelike state in which we can easily feel helpless and hopeless."[5] I can certainly attest to having experienced those emotions in relation to the world I live in, especially as I've witnessed the slow but steady push to normalize practices like pedophilia, bestiality, and cannibalism in the entertainment industry. From this point of view, not only do we have the right to question our society's predominant value system, we have the obligation to do so. It's an integral part of our becoming aware and of learning to value the truth of our own experience and our own knowing. It's also an integral part of our living a life of our own choosing.

I suggest that the first step in becoming conscious and honoring your own truth is to tune in to what you *feel* in your body—your visceral sensations and emotions. Please pay close attention to how your body resonates when you hear or read the thoughts and beliefs of others, especially of those in positions of authority. Do their words elicit feelings of peacefulness and compassion or do you feel riled up and angry, full of contempt for those who are perceived to be different from you? Do you feel uplifted by the words and the emotion behind them or do you feel somehow that something's just not right?

My barometer of the energy that's around me is my stomach. When my stomach contracts and hurts, I know that something is out of balance, and I need to pay close attention. In an ideal world we would be taught as children to recognize and value our intuition. We'd be taught to pay attention to how our bodies register and process feelings. We'd also be taught to automatically question those people who have set themselves up as authority figures and who claim to know what's best for us. We'd be instructed to do this even if we felt that what was being presented was already part of our world view. In many instances, the people we need to examine and question most carefully are the ones we've already agreed with and have come to trust, since we tend to assume, often incorrectly, that they will always represent our best interests.

Becoming cognizant of exactly which values guide our everyday living may seem unnecessary and even scary at first, since it represents the need to *ask questions* about the beliefs and assumptions on which we've based our entire lives. The problem is that some of the assumptions we've learned to make about ourselves and about life in general constrict and constrain us and cause us suffering. And they're usually not wholly conscious. In *The Third Millennium: Living in the Post Historic World*, Ken Carey suggests that matter holds its spell over us through language, and that "belief systems are illusions of linguistically structured thought... They are cages created by words, imprisoning their makers."[6] Thus, based on which family and which culture we're brought up in, we may harbor half-conscious, restrictive beliefs about life and ourselves such as, I'm not as worthy as someone else because I don't have their money or status or looks. Or I don't deserve good things because I'm inherently bad. Or I can't express vulnerability because it's not safe and it's an indication of weakness. After we identify what our major presumptions are about ourselves and life, we can see how we may be creating our own lives by acting out our core beliefs and self-images.

Once we start to uncover how our behavior reflects what we believe, we begin to understand that we have a certain degree of personal responsibility for our own lives. And with personal responsibility comes the potential for action and change. Unfortunately most of us have been raised to conform indiscriminately to the norms of our group and to be afraid of change of any kind. At this stage in humanity's history, however, even if we decide to not make outward changes, we are still being challenged to become conscious of the beliefs and feelings that actually motivate us. In the end, the ultimate goal of our questioning is to bring an end to our suffering, and compassionate self-awareness is the first step.

If we do make changes in our behavior, we may encounter immense resistance from others to our living out our own reality and our refusing to conform. It can take great *courage* to listen to and honor the inner voice that speaks to you of your own truth. I know firsthand the fear that can come up when we go against intense group pressure, and I know the strength it takes to stand alone. It can be a painful experience to be censured and lose friends because you're going against the consensus of your group. I've taken comfort in remembering the words of the great Frederick Douglass in his *Narrative of the Life of Frederick Douglass*, "I prefer to be true to myself, even at the hazard of incurring ridicule from others, rather than to be false and incur my own abhorrence."[7] But while we do have the obligation to know and to honor what our own experience reveals to us, I ask that, even as you may question another's truth, you allow yourself the possibility of keeping an open mind while you sample someone else's version of reality. It's important that we not dismiss out of hand any truth or wisdom that may be held within another's perspective, since a different perspective may permit different shades of the truth to be revealed.

Each of us comes to life with an underlying soul purpose, often felt as some unnamable, inchoate longing of the heart. Each of us has unique gifts to give in service to the life of the world, and the world is waiting for us to be absolutely, uniquely ourselves. Life is waiting for you to be only *yourself*. I love the old Hasidic story of the rabbi who dies and goes to heaven. He tells God that all his life he did the best he could to be like Moses. With some dismay God replies, "But I didn't want you to be more like Moses. I wanted you to be more like *yourself*."

Many of us cannot easily access the memory of what our gift or purpose is, given the fact that the world we live in rarely supports the goal of the individual's awakening. Through the experiences of our lives, however, through the triumphs and the joys, the heartbreak and disappointments, and through just letting "the soft animal of your body love what it loves" (Mary Oliver, from her poem, *Wild Geese*[8]), we are led back to the memory of that original longing and purpose. We are led back through the whispers from our true Self. And until we remember what gifts we came to give or what wildness we came to unfold, we will feel unsatisfied and out of place in the world. In her amazing, love-filled *Inspired and Unstoppable: Wildly Succeeding in Your Life's Work*, Tama Kieves gives expression to the need to not deny our deepest gifts and to live out our wildest dreams:

> "It's eventually unbearable to deny our love, strength, and essence. We've said 'yes' to some sacred arrangement in the ethers, and here on earth—until we live our most meaningful dreams—we ache with the pangs of blessings unfulfilled."[9]

Throughout the years I've had many opportunities to *test out through my own deep experience,* and through what resonates in me of others' experience, the reality of what I present to you here. With the "gift" of each challenge or crisis in my life (and, yes, some gifts come poorly wrapped!), Spirit has proven to me that I am never alone or unsupported or unloved. Each time, Spirit has pursued me and won me over with its love and steadfastness, even when I was too gripped by fear to be very receptive. It will do the same for you if you can open your mind and heart, even just a little, to the undreamed-of possibilities and blessings that Spirit is waiting to give you.

I have written this book to give you the opportunity to experience the same force of unconditional love that I first felt for myself that long-ago July afternoon. Please take a risk and open yourself to the reality of the love coming to you and within you now, the love that Spirit so dearly wants you to feel.

Spirit is speaking to us now, to you ...

*Dear One, can you allow for this possibility...that this Great Spirit of All That is and All That Can Be loves you so dearly, loves you beyond your human understanding—not for how much money you have or how many friends you can claim or what position you hold. This Great Spirit of All That Can Be loves you beyond what words can know because you exist – and your existence is a **uniquely beautiful** and magnificent expression of this love.*

*It is time, Dear One, to remember that you can rely on the quiet, inner voice of your own higher self, your connection to Great Spirit. It is time to allow yourself to know and to feel your **own wild truth** and honor it.*

*The love that is coming to you, the love that you **are**, is the very fabric of your being. Let this love be your foundation, your grounding, as you make the daring journey of sharing the astonishing beauty of your authentic self with the world.*

CHAPTER III

Awakening—to the Reality of Love

The dust of many crumbled cities
Settles over us like a forgetful doze,
But we are older than those cities

Rumi[1]

The Concept of Awakening

We are now in the midst of the most extraordinary and far-reaching awakening of consciousness that this planet has ever witnessed. It is a time of transformation and changing paradigms that began in 1987, over the days of August 16th and 17th, with an exceptional planetary alignment referred to as the Harmonic Convergence. I was not aware at that time that the Harmonic Convergence was an event, inspired by Dr. José Arguelles, to celebrate the acceleration of energy and the raising of consciousness on the earth. In the weeks leading up to the Convergence, however, I read that many people were going to meditate at dawn on these days, especially at sacred sites around the world. I wanted to be part of honoring the auspicious planetary event even though I was not consciously aware of its deeper significance, and I planned to greet the dawn in solidarity with the others around the world.

I remember the morning of August 17th very well. My mother was enthusiastic about joining me in meditation so I went to her home the night before. She had a small house (the home I had grown up in) with a backyard patio that faced east. We sat outside just before daybreak and felt the quiet beauty and special energy of the hour. Red roses and honeysuckle and lily of the valley were blooming, and the cool early morning air was filled with heavenly scents. We sat together in the stillness and witnessed the gradual rising of the sun through the branches of the trees beyond the yard. The first rays of the sun were glorious and we closed our eyes with a sense of peace as we silently blessed the earth.

As I understand it there were many of us at the time of the Convergence who either consciously or on a soul level, made the commitment to awaken to the deeper reality of love as the substrate of all of life. In so doing, a critical mass of group consciousness had been reached. From that day forward there could be no reversing the tide of the awakening. *We had done it* and there was tremendous joy in the universe! When the final phase of this rebirthing process comes to an end many years from now, we will have succeeded in building a veritable heaven on earth. This heaven on earth will be based on spiritual principles, the greatest of which is the power of compassion and love to heal the wounds of our inner and outer worlds.

Planetary awakening is happening through *us,* one mind and one heart at a time. On a soul level, you and I and everyone else on the earth have agreed to participate, either directly or indirectly, in the waking up of human (and nonhuman!) consciousness. We could hardly wait to come back to the physical plane to be here at this cosmically historic time. Please know that you are an integral part of this incredible process of change. Your participation is necessary, and you already have everything you need to participate in and contribute to the awakening.

The Waking Dream

Have you ever had a bad dream, a nightmare, which was so vivid and real that when you awoke from it you were relieved that it was just a dream—that it wasn't real? Perhaps you woke up with your heart pounding from intense fear. The experience of the nightmare felt as real as any experience you've ever had while you were awake. So which is the real experience—the dreaming one or the waking one?

In a way, both experiences are real at different levels. It's just that one state of consciousness (the so-called awake one) gives us a larger perspective on what is real; it gives us a more inclusive understanding. (It should be noted, however, that there are some who believe that the *sleeping* dream is more real than the awake one.) We are able to perceive and understand that there is more than one level or dimension of our experiencing. We might say, "Oh yes, that dream I had was so real that had I not awakened, I might have believed it was the only reality. Now that I'm awake I'm able to see that the dreaming state is just one level of awareness. There exist other levels of awareness, other states of consciousness that I can access." Of course even within the sleeping dream state, there are other possible levels of awareness, as exemplified by the phenomenon of lucid dreaming, where the dreamer is aware that he or she is dreaming. There's also the concept of dream work, where it is believed that the dreaming mind works with higher spiritual energies.

What if the experience of full, waking consciousness were itself another kind of dream state, a "waking dream?" In the waking dream, we're awake to a certain extent; that is, we're not sleeping. But we're not fully conscious and cognizant of what the deeper reality is beneath the appearance of things. We're dreaming a kind of dream but unaware that we're dreaming until we've learned to access other states of awareness.

There are higher levels of consciousness in which one is more awake and aware than in the normal waking state. In these "superconscious" states we can feel and access the deeper, unseen spiritual reality of life. We can experience what Buddhism refers to as our "Buddha-nature," our already awakened nature. As consciousness is transformed, humankind is beginning to *wake up from even the waking dream* to remember the truth of who we really are—that we are part of Spirit and not separate from it. We're beginning to remember that we are powerful, spiritual, co-creating *partners* with the divine, co-creating our lives one belief and one thought and one desire at a time.

One of my favorite stories is about Chuang Tsu, a Chinese Taoist philosopher, who is believed to have lived in the second half of the fourth century B.C.E. He dreamt that he was a butterfly, fluttering here and there, conscious only of his happiness as a butterfly, unaware that he was Chuang Tsu. When he awoke from his dream he marveled at how real it had felt. After contemplating the dream experience he wondered which state was real: Am I a man dreaming I'm a butterfly or am I a butterfly dreaming I'm a man? It's a useful question to ask ourselves—just who exactly is it who is dreaming these dreams? *Who are we? Who are you?* Who is it who believes he or she is awake but is really dreaming the waking dream? Perhaps we are angels who are dreaming that we are human and who have chosen this time in history to truly wake up from that dream in the midst of the world's illusions.

I Offer You ...

I offer you what I have come to realize and understand from my own experience through the process of awakening; I offer you the possibility ...

that *you are dearly loved* not for what you possess or accomplish but simply because you exist, and because your very existence is the joyful expression of divine love. Neither is love withdrawn from you for what you say or do or neglect to say or do. Love cannot be withdrawn from you; *it is who you are.* Divine love is your essence, your core. It is the essence of all beings, even though there are external differences among us.

This love can be likened to the life-giving light that shines from the sun. The dazzling light shines freely on all of the earth while only its appearance is changed by the filters through which it passes. The same sunlight is perceived differently when seen through clouds or dust in the air or at the varied angles at which the light strikes the earth. Filtered through stained glass, for example, sunlight takes on the patterned appearance of the design of the glass. Each design, with its different colors and shapes, changes the look of the light, while the source and quality of the light remain unchanged. The different designs are screens or modifiers through which the one light is expressed; the essence of light itself does not change. The same principle applies to the light of divine love expressing itself through the magnificent and unique filters of our individuality, actually through the filters of all of creation. At our **core** you and I and all beings are the same brilliant light of divine love.

All that you see and hear and feel, All That Is and All That Can Be, is the creative expression of the living, conscious light and energy of divine love, whether that love is perceived as physical form (light-energy condensed to a slow vibration) or is unseen and form*less*. All That Is and All That Can Be is the energy of an ineffable and infinite higher love. Indeed, the light of divine love is the "substance" at the heart of the atoms and the molecules that comprise your body and your physical world.

Your consciousness is infinite and eternal—and is inexorably linked to all other consciousness, to all other beings. This connection exists as a unified energy field—a network of interwoven vibrational patterns that is indivisible and indestructible. If one tiny cell in the field is affected, there is a rippling out of energy that can subtly change all the cells of the field. This interconnection among all living things means that your energy can and does affect the energy and consciousness of everyone else in the world in subtle and sometimes not so subtle ways. Implied in this interconnection is the fact that you have the power to effect real change in the world, first and foremost, by loving and healing yourself.

Spirit is speaking to you now through me ...

*Beloved, you are sacred because you are the living **embodiment** of an immeasurable, unfathomable love. You are this love in form, and* *your focused consciousness is so potentially powerful that any change of heart you can allow, any emotional healing that you may choose, like forgiveness or compassion, starting with yourself, can and does affect the entire unified energy field of the planet!*

*Can you imagine it, Dear One? Can you imagine that **your** healing of **your** heart can and does affect the hearts of all beings in creation? As the embodiment of a love beyond what you can comprehend, you are so significant and so powerful that your healing alone could conceivably tip the balance of energy from dark to light—from fear and hatred to compassion and gentleness—on the earth. You are awakening to the truth of this now, Beloved, and all is well.*

As Your Consciousness Awakens ...

I offer you the possibility that we existed as consciousness before this physical lifetime, and that we continue to exist, without our physical body, after this life. Our consciousness is continuous and never ending. Just as energy cannot be destroyed, only changed in form, so our consciousness cannot die. You may wonder why we don't remember this when we're here on the physical plane. As I understand it, we don't remember when we incarnate because, with so little knowledge and support of the spiritual truth of life from the world around us, our memories quickly begin to fade until there is no conscious awareness of what lies beyond the "veil." Essentially this is the power of the so-called consensus reality of society, embraced by those we depend upon for our very survival when we are little.

At this stage in our evolution if we did remember our true identity and the true nature of reality from birth forward, there would be no lessons to be learned, no truth to be uncovered, and no illusions to cut through. We would already know that all beings are part of the divine and are intimately connected to one another. We would already know that our divine legacy is to love and to consciously create. From another perspective, if we did know the truth from birth onward, there would not be the immeasurable joy of our homecoming, of our discovering within what we've been searching for all along.

The physical world is a challenging place and, in my reality, we know this before we "sign on" to come here through many lifetimes. We know full well that we can get lost in and seduced by all the beauty and sensuality of the material world. We know that the world will almost certainly overwhelm us, that we will forget our origins, our purpose, that we will forget our divine identity as part of the living light. We know that the world will distract us from the knowledge that we are dearly loved and *that we are love itself.*

Thus, you and I are considered by Spirit to be nothing short of heroes just for coming into the world while knowing that we will most likely not remember who we really are. We are heroes simply because we chose to come into the uncertainty of physical existence with nothing but the highest form of love, the highest of motivations: to unfold spiritually and to continue to bear witness to this unfathomable love that is our essence. As we do our unfolding and healing, we help to heal the consciousness of all others and thus bring the living planet into an exquisite vibrational space of love and peace. This idea may sound like a fantasy, but it's not. It's a reality that you and I are now dreaming into glorious being.

Changing Paradigms

A major aspect of the awakening and transformation of consciousness now taking place is the world-wide shift of paradigms. Slowly but surely, as we awaken from the waking dream, we see the old model of living coming to an end. That model involved our living unconscious and fear-based lives, unaware of the presence and power of infinite love. It involved our giving away our power to know and to understand to some external authority. As the world shifts away from the old ways of thinking, we are acknowledging and releasing our fears, and in so doing, beginning to remember that we already have the inherent capacity to access divine wisdom and to co-create as *partners* with the creative force of Spirit.

The old paradigm was exemplified by the belief that we didn't have and couldn't have direct access to the divine. We were taught that we needed some kind of mediator, such as a member of the clergy or a recognized guru or shaman, between us and Spirit. The truth is that you and I have never needed a mediator since we are already part of Spirit. I do understand, however, that there can be substantial benefits from a relationship with a mature spiritual teacher. The benefits can come from reading the teacher's writings or from hearing the teacher speak. Sometimes just being in the presence of an enlightened soul can cause a quantum leap of understanding and awakening in a student. There are many stories, historical and contemporary, of how a spiritual apprentice has realized the love that is the divine Self through an ongoing and deep relationship with a trusted teacher. Transpersonal psychologist, John Welwood, suggests that the presence of a genuine spiritual teacher can,

> "serve as a mirror that reflects back to students qualities of their **awakened** being: openness, generosity, discernment, humor, gentleness, acceptance, compassion, straightforwardness, strength and courage."[2] [emphasis added]

But he makes a distinction between mindful surrender and mindless submission to a teacher and their teachings. Mindful surrender involves opening to deeper aspects of truth, while mindless submission represents a "deadening flight from freedom."[3] Sharon

Salzberg offers similar insights into the issue in her book on faith. She suggests that with a teacher who has made a commitment to realizing spiritual truth, their "urgency to be truthful, to wake up, to not waste their lives can light a sense of urgency in us as well."[4] At the same time she cautions that when we put our faith completely in others instead of in our own experience and understanding, "we end up caught in the shadow side of surrender and devotion."[5]

Since the essence of the Sanskrit word "guru" is "heavy with spiritual knowledge" and implies someone who dispels the darkness of spiritual ignorance, we can go beyond the formal teacher-student model to discover that anyone and everyone has the potential to serve as guru to us. Hinduism even has a term, *upaguru*, which refers to the guru next to you. As long as we are paying attention, anyone or any set of circumstances can open our eyes to some truth and to some wisdom that we had not seen before. My sister, Joan, remembers a poignant experience with an *upaguru* once when she as at home recovering from major surgery. Feeling overwhelmed by the many professional and family responsibilities and challenges facing her, she'd call on her faith and give the outcome of all her issues to God. After a while, though, she'd slip back into fear and worry. One day, a lovely woman who was her temporary housekeeper asked her, "You know what's wrong with you, honey? I'll tell you what's wrong with you. You may give everything to God, but then you think He's not doing a good job so you take it all back!" Her words jarred my sister into remembering that you either trust in God's benevolence and support or you don't. She decided to trust. Whomever we look to for spiritual guidance, however, we need to remember that our gurus sometimes have feet of clay, and ultimately we must trust what we feel when we go into that centered and quiet place within ourselves.

As the awakening of consciousness gathers momentum, people all over the world are allowing themselves to question their old beliefs and question the dogma of their religions and their political affiliations. They're questioning their participation in any social group that requires them to conform to rigid interpretations of reality. They're asking themselves whether their beliefs ultimately encourage them to be more compassionate, more loving, and more aware. Sometimes the answer is no.

I honor and respect all sincere means of seeking and connecting with the divine, whether that entails being part of an organized religion or part of a spiritually oriented community or not being part of a group at all. If we do choose an organized religion as our spiritual path, it's useful to remember that most of the world's religions have sacred texts and that there is wisdom and truth to be found in all of them. As we continue to awaken we will need to move beyond the differences among religions' scriptures and focus on the core of the messages in each, which most often turns out to be one of kindness and self-awareness. In addition to reading scripture, however, I do ask that you take a risk, at least once in a while, to put down your spiritual books and sacred texts, and allow yourself to be drawn into the silence within. Going to that place of innate intuition, to the still and quiet spaciousness within yourself, you can ask, What is real? What is my truth? And Who am I really? These are really the only questions that matter.

Another aspect of the old paradigm, at least for some, is the complete dependence on religious text as the *only means* of revealing spiritual truth and the divine. This has begun to change, slowly but surely. The remarkable philosopher, Jacob Needleman, has spoken about finding the wonder of God in places other than scripture such as the stars in the night sky and,

> "the extraordinary beauty of nature …What I see out there awakens an impersonal joy within me, as if this wonder is what I really am, rather than being my day to day self, which we can call 'ego.'…

This gift comes from God, and anyone can have it, without religious trappings."[6]

For some people, of course, the wonder and spirituality they have in their lives is not related to the concept of a God at all. Many find joy and truth and transcendence in things like the love we share with those close to us, including our companion animals, or in the beauty of a piece of music or a painting, or in the rapturous song of the Wood Thrush.

With the changing of paradigms, perhaps it's time for humanity as a whole to begin to wonder about how we have come to believe what we believe. Perhaps it's time for us to wonder how we can be certain that everything that was written centuries or millennia ago is the ultimate truth. How can we be sure that it is *our* truth? Why have we been taught to believe *anything* without questioning? Some might say that they believe what they believe because of the traditions of the religion into which they were born. That's an understandable response. However, because a religious custom is passed down through generations, does not automatically make it sacred nor necessarily mean that it's based on the reality of love. A tradition does not automatically reflect one's own heart-felt truth or even, for that matter, a loving response to the world. There are some religious traditions that demonstrate a true lack of regard for human and nonhuman life, and some appear to celebrate retribution. Albert Einstein's reputed quote, "A foolish faith in authority is the worst enemy of truth"[7] holds true not only for religion but also for the realms of politics, education, medicine, and basically for all areas of life.

I offer you the possibility that whatever is of lasting value in any literature is already within your deeper self, your connection to the divine. Whatever is of ultimate truth in any book of scripture, that truth—and more—has already been written by Spirit in your own beautiful heart. In her poem, *The Summer Day*, Pulitzer Prize-winner, Mary Oliver, asks, "what is it you plan to do with your one wild and precious life?"[8] I do not believe that we are meant to live our *wild* and precious lives on automatic pilot, never daring to question the status quo, never daring to disobey the rules put down by our families and our societal institutions. Can you take that risk of letting go of your doctrinal and scriptural security blankets, at least once in a while, to explore the richness of what may be found in the silence within you?

As we awaken and evolve, it is our own deeply experienced truth that we must honor as our guiding principle. Now is the time to go into the still center within ourselves—and listen. We will eventually come to realize that we already have access to everything we'll ever need to know. We will come to realize that we have the capability to know as much as any authority figure knows, as much as any living saint or sage knows. We have just forgotten, to varying degrees, that we can access this knowing. In *The Third Millennium*, Ken Carey interprets Spirit's words for us, "Do not short-circuit your life energy by trying to work on, change, or improve your grasp of the truth. Begin trusting the truth I have created in you, *the truth that you yourself are.*"[9]

Within this new paradigm of reclaiming our ability to be aware and to co-create consciously, I offer you a further possibility that, in a world that is waking up, perhaps even the age-old concept of worship may take on new meaning for us. If divine love is already our innate nature and our essence, then perhaps we are meant only to *honor* that love and *celebrate* its presence in ourselves and in all beings instead of worshipping a distant deity that is considered completely separate from us. Perhaps we are meant to rejoice in the presence and expression of this divinity—this profound love—within ourselves and within all of creation, and then live our lives in accordance with this knowledge. Ultimately, we're being asked to turn within ourselves to find what Buddhism has called the "jewel in the heart of the lotus," the Godhead in ourselves, that is waiting to be remembered. I had a dream once that helped me understand this on a profound level…

Looking for Gold

Years ago I was initiated into a tribe of the Lakota nation. The teacher who initiated me is a revered healer, one who's called an antelope, and he began by asking me to go into a deep meditative state and tell the story of my life's path. He told me that at some point I would receive a sign from Spirit if I had been accepted into the tribe. I wasn't told what the sign would be but he would confirm it if I saw it. Toward the end of recounting my life's journey, in my mind's eye I saw a strong young Native American man ride by me on a beautiful Pinto horse. He shot an arrow right into my heart and it seemed to create an explosion of light. That vision was the confirmation of my being accepted. My teacher also told me that the driving rain that had begun during my initiation was a sign that I was being blessed.

After the initiation was complete, my teacher told me to watch my dreams closely that night. He said that I would have a significant dream, and possibly a revelation within the dream. I went to sleep that night with excitement, anticipating some sort of personal message from Spirit. The dream that I experienced that night *was* significant, but not only for me; it was significant for you as well. It spoke about the treasure of Spirit within each one of us.

I dreamt that I was in an underground jewelry store that was beneath Grand Central Station in New York City. There were no windows or views of the outside. I was looking intently for gold jewelry for myself, gold earrings in particular. Many pairs of earrings were displayed in those revolving display cases that you see in some stores, but I couldn't find anything I liked. Each pair of earrings that I picked up and examined closely was somehow a disappointment. Some of earrings were solid gold but they weren't beautifully designed, while others were only gold-plated. What's more, the gold plating had begun to wear off and there were patches of base metal showing through.

I put down the last pair of earrings and was about to give up on finding something of beauty, when all of a sudden, I realized that there was something in my mouth. I could feel several small objects on my tongue which had to have come from within me, since I hadn't put anything in my mouth. I gently spit out the objects into the palm of my left hand, and I was stunned to see what was there. In my hand were several pieces of exquisite diamonds and many tiny and perfect double-terminated crystals. The beauty and brilliance and rainbow shimmer of the diamonds and crystals far outshone the flawed gold jewelry around me.

I woke up then and began to realize what the dream was trying to help me remember: that my search, that *our* search, for external beauty and riches is misguided and backwards. The wealth and the magnificence that we so desperately seek are already within us, *underground*, as it were, under the surface of our experience and our conditioning. What we search for outside of ourselves pales in comparison to the store of richness at the divine core of our being and at the core of every being. When you turn to the treasure within, you can access Spirit's brilliant clarity (deep knowing) and beauty (endless, tender compassion and joy) as part of your own original nature, because the jewel in the heart of the lotus *is already within your own shimmering heart.*

What if we'd been taught from childhood that the beauty and goodness of Spirit were within us, that this was our very nature and essence? What if we'd been taught that our essence retained an imprint of divine perfection, the memory of which resided within the soul?

Wouldn't that have changed everything? *What if it were true?*

Spirit is coming through now to speak to us, to you and me...

Dear One, you are a magnificent and radiant soul in the midst of an awakening and transformation of consciousness the likes of which this planet has never seen before. Your intention and your courage to awaken is attracting Beings of Light from all over the cosmos. Filled with awe and wonder over you, they are flying to you on angels' wings to honor you and support you. Right this moment you are being cherished and cheered on by the forces of Light in all of creation. You are so dearly loved. Can you imagine it?

Beloved, please know that you have come into this world with infinite consciousness and access to the deep wisdom of Spirit. Thus you have everything you need to be awake and happy. It's all there within you, within your own amazing, light-filled heart.

Beings of Light are showering you and all beings with blessings now and always.

CHAPTER IV

Seeing Through the Illusions

I wish I could speak like music.

I wish I could put the swaying splendor
Of the fields into words

So that you could hold Truth
Against your body
And dance.

Hafiz[1]

A Spiritual Perspective on "Development"

Many of us suffer from deep insecurities and self-doubt because we've never been taught that not only are we cherished by an infinite source of love, we actually *are* this energy of love in form. We've never understood that we *are* inherent goodness. So it's understandable that we may wonder how we can come to trust that we are loved and that we are love itself. With this in mind, I offer some thoughts on the concept of development.

The fundamental nature of your being, your *essence*, is the fire and light of divine love, and it cannot be extinguished nor destroyed. This beautiful and radiant light of love shone in your heart the moment you were born, and it still shines there, even if you can't remember it. Since your essence is your true identity, then development, instead of implying self-improvement, would really mean becoming conscious of the layers of erroneous beliefs about yourself and the world that have congealed around and concealed your forgotten light. I suggest to you that there is no one else you need to be but just who you already are—beneath the conditioned self-images that are the masks the ego wears.

The essence of your heart has not changed since the moment of your birth, but there are good reasons why we're all prone to forget this truth. As we are socialized throughout childhood, we are gradually exposed to ever deeper levels of unawakened conditioning from our families, from mass media, and from the major cultural institutions that form the foundation of our society. This programming often ends up encouraging us (in subtle and not so subtle ways) to feel fearful and inadequate and not worthy of love. Thus some of us come out of childhood feeling the need to keep up a steady stream of accomplishments in order to stave off the feeling of not being good enough and to try to prove our worth to ourselves and others. We may feel that we have to keep improving ourselves in many ways just to be okay.

Most of us are not taught to ask questions about what serves or doesn't serve our unfolding as emotional and spiritual beings. We often grow up accepting uncritically our family's social and religious traditions and our culture's normative heritage: the party line, so to speak, of our material existence. We are *conditioned* to believe in certain values, to make certain assumptions, and many of us never dare to question official versions of reality. Often we're not even aware that there are questions to be asked or layers of conditioning to be examined!

Such a state of affairs implies a deeply habituated conformity of thinking, a process of selective perception and an unconsciously agreed-upon passivity of the intellect. This "consensus trance," as transpersonal psychologist, Charles Tart, has referred to it, is the basis for our forgetting about the very existence of the light within us. So our essence, that light at the core, gets covered over by layers of illusions representing years' worth of false self-images and misassumptions about the very nature of reality. With layer upon layer, veil upon veil, the light at the center that is our deepest reality is obscured. This consensus trance is an energetic imprint that shapes our fundamental beliefs about who we are and about what we think is real—and therefore what we think is even *possible*—throughout our entire lifetime. So if we're not even aware of the basic goodness of our authentic self to begin with, we can go through our entire lives never remembering who we really are.

Since it is *awareness* that begins our healing, only by paying loving attention to our erroneous and often semi-conscious beliefs and feelings and how they manifest in our lives, can we begin to become conscious of our true Self. Only with compassionate awareness— gentle, nonjudgmental attention—and the willingness to release beliefs that no longer serve us, can we start the healing process. Then we can gradually drop the layers, one by one, exposing the light of love that has always been at the center of the heart.

The spiritual perspective on development speaks ultimately of not having to become a better person, of not having to become a "new and improved version of yourself." It's not possible to improve on the essence—it's already the perfection of divine love and awakened consciousness. The spiritual perspective speaks of giving yourself permission *to relax into who you already are, at heart.*

Examining the Illusions

The beliefs that a society agrees upon are internalized as our own, without question for the most part. During the current transformation of consciousness, however, we are beginning to awaken from the sleep of being caught up in illusory beliefs about ourselves and the nature of the physical world. Specifically, these illusions are created from what we're able to see and hear and touch in the world around us. For example, what we can see tells us that all beings are separated from each other by space, that we are all distinct, completely independent and disconnected beings. Albert Einstein called this "a kind of optical delusion of consciousness."[2] In spiritual reality however, in the reality that most of us cannot see with our physical eyes, no true separation exists, and all beings are *energy fields* continually interacting with all other energy fields. Using only the data from our limited physical senses, we believe that we are mortal and separate and sometimes powerless beings, while the unseen and more profound reality is to the contrary. What's more, there is growing evidence that *our very sense perceptions are shaped and conditioned as part of our being acculturated.*

Shared beliefs about what is real in the world—and even more importantly—about what is *possible*—gradually shape our experiences and eventually undermine our ability to perceive other realities that would not be accepted as true by the group. *Our very ability to sense the range of perceptual stimuli is limited by the culture's tacit consensus on what is considered real and unreal in life.* We can see examples of this every once in a while with young children who are able to perceive beings in other dimensions. Some little ones can even remember scenes and details from their past lives, sometimes giving verifiable information about a former lifetime. The adults around them, though, often tell them that what they see and feel isn't real and that they're imagining what they're experiencing. Before long most of these children stop perceiving anything beyond what is sanctioned by their social environment. Author and investigative reporter, Jon Rappoport, suggests that reality has been co-opted,

> "What has been called The Matrix is a series of layers. These layers compose what we call Reality. Reality is not merely the consensus people accept in their daily lives. It is also a personal and individual conception of limits. It is a perception that these limits are somehow built into existence. But this is not true."[3]

Apropos of this, author and Emmy-winner Dick Cavett has written about how he and an elder member of the Crow Nation once stood high above the battlefield where the bloody battle of Wounded Knee had been fought in 1876. Cavett recounted to the elder how he'd been there one night by himself and had hoped to catch a glimpse of ghostly figures from the battle. Taking a moment before commenting, the elder responded, "Those things are always there. It's just that you have learned not to see them." Cavett added, "Our loss."[4]

The concept of death is a major example of a programmed illusion. When someone we know dies, because of our limited capacity to perceive anything outside the realm of visible light, we may believe that they're gone forever. The underlying reality, however, is that there is no death. The physical vehicle dies, but our consciousness doesn't die; it's just released from form. I like the analogy of renting a car in this regard. The rented car is our body, the vehicle for the soul's journey, and our consciousness and energy are the driver. It's as if we pick up the car that we'd reserved when we're born into the world and we drive it for the length of the lifetime. When we've finished with our vehicle we return it to the rental agent. In the material world we all understand that we are not the actual car that we rent; someday we will all understand that we are not only our physical bodies either. My own experiences have given me much evidence of the survival of the spirit after death.

Although I'm not a classic medium and I usually receive only limited messages, I have connected many times with the consciousness of those who have passed over. A consistent theme of their communication is that they want us to know that they are still alive and still with us. One of my favorite examples of these occasions was with a young woman client named Jackie M. She and her family have given me permission to tell their story.

Jackie's much loved father, Johnny, had just died after a very brief battle with lung cancer, and she, her mother, Virginia, and her sister, Lori, were devastated. When I met with Jackie for the first time after her Dad's death she asked if we could meditate and pray and talk to her Dad's spirit. She hoped that I might receive a message or sign from him. She and her family wanted some kind of evidence that there was life after death and they wanted to make sure that he was all right. After briefly tuning in to Johnny's energy he came through loud and clear with specific and personal images for Jackie and her mother.

For Jackie the message was an image of a head of cauliflower! When I told her what I'd been shown she was crestfallen. She had no idea what a simple picture of cauliflower could mean. She pondered the image for a minute and then she gasped. She remembered that just a few hours before, while on her lunch break from her job, she had spoken aloud to her Dad about cauliflower! That day she'd gotten a steamed vegetable bowl for lunch at the local health food restaurant, and she noticed that there was much more cauliflower in the mix than usual. Sitting in her car as she ate, the extra cauliflower reminded her of her Dad and she smiled. Speaking to him out loud while chuckling she said, "I love cauliflower and so did you, Dad. I know you loved cauliflower so much, but of course *you* preferred Mom's breaded and fried cauliflower! You probably never even tasted steamed cauliflower." The fact that her Dad acknowledged her speaking to him that day about cauliflower was enough to convince Jackie that he was present with her, and she was overjoyed at the communication between them. She said that her Dad's message had given her comfort and reassurance and had helped her to begin to heal her grief.

The message for Jackie's mom, Virginia, was also a visual one of her putting on a red sweater. It turned out that she had worn a red sweater that day. Over their years together Johnny would admire and compliment Virginia whenever she wore red, so she was not surprised that he would comment on the red clothing. Jackie and I were disappointed, though, that no message had come through for Lori, Jackie's younger sister.

Lori, a junior in high school at the time, was understandably upset that she had not yet received any sign or message from her father. The next time I met with Jackie I tried again. Tuning in to Johnny's spirit I asked him for a personal message for his other daughter. This time there were no images, just the sound of the words, "skate key." I wondered to myself, "What the heck is this?" I hadn't heard the term skate key for decades and no one I knew roller skated anymore. For the longest time I remained quiet while silently asking Johnny to confirm and explain what he had said. The response was the same two words. I finally told Jackie that the message didn't make any sense to me but here it was, skate key. She wasn't pleased with the answer and I couldn't blame her.

I didn't hear from Jackie for a few weeks so I assumed that Lori had found the message meaningless. Then one day she called to tell me that it had taken her all that time to tell anyone what her father's message for Lori had been since she thought it just too far out to be authentic. She had thought, "How can I tell this poor girl who's grieving that strange message when there's probably nothing to it?" But one day she finally decided to describe the message to her mother during a phone conversation. Her mother quickly relayed the words to her other daughter who was nearby. Lori was silent for a few moments and then she let out a scream and sat down on the landing of the stairs, crying and yelling from shock and joy. She had understood the message.

Around the time that her father had given me the message, Lori's English class had been discussing the novel, *Catcher in the Rye*. The teacher was talking about a scene from the book where the protagonist tightens a child's roller skate with a skate key. From the discussion of the skate key in the novel the teacher then segued into a lengthy tangent about the skate key he'd had when he was young! With Johnny's message of "skate key" he was letting Lori know that he had been in the classroom with her during that tangent. That knowledge gave her and Jackie and Virginia great comfort. Actually Jackie has told me that Johnny's messages have continued to give them solace and hope over the years.

Another of my favorite examples of communicating with the other side are the messages received from my mother. Over the years since my mother passed there have been many communications from her, beginning on the day of her funeral. Family members had flown in or driven in to attend the memorial and the burial.

As they made preparations to leave, we all decided that we would ask Mom (and Grandmother and Great Grandmother) to give us the sight of a rainbow as a sign that her spirit was still with us. Later that day as they were all driving south on the New Jersey Turnpike, I got an excited call from my niece with unbelievable news. She said that across the southern sky in front of them were not one but two huge rainbows! We chose to interpret the sight of those rainbows as evidence that Mom was still alive even though she had left her body.

A few years after my mother's passing I was walking my precious dog, Belle Esther, on the city streets where I lived. There were tears in my eyes as I walked in the unseasonably cold drizzle of an early October afternoon. I was hurting over a difficult love relationship and feeling alone. I said aloud, "Mimi (that was the nickname she'd chosen for herself after my father died), if you can hear me I could really use the comfort of knowing you're with me now. Can you show me your rainbow?"

For several blocks I searched the patches of grey sky between the tall buildings in every direction except to the east. There was an open expanse of sky to the east but I couldn't see it just yet because buildings were blocking the view. For half an hour I looked to the sky but no rainbow appeared. Nothing. I was feeling dejected.

Then just as Belle and I turned the corner and headed east to go home, I saw it. Over the tree tops, the sky had begun to clear and was showing off the largest, most beautiful, shimmering rainbow I'd ever seen. I just stood there, filled with relief and gratitude, and I photographed the rainbow with my phone just before it disappeared.

One communication with consciousness on the other side was unexpected and quite dramatic. When I lived in Chapel Hill, NC,

I made it a point to attend a monthly gathering called the "Bliss Café." The event was intended to help participants experience bliss and was presented by two radiant Lightworkers, Lauren Jubilirer, energy healer and acupuncturist, and Daran Wallman, mystic and extraordinary musician. During the event Lauren placed small acupuncture needles in our ear lobes at the points associated with the feeling of bliss. Daran created the energy of bliss with his gift of playing the didgeridoo, an instrument that has always felt sacred to me. When Daran played his instrument I could feel the healing vibration of the sound moving through my whole being. It was numinous and ethereal. In this out-of-this-world state I sometimes heard the word "Dreamtime," and it felt like I was back at the beginning of time.

During one of these sessions, as the sound and the effect of the acupuncture took me to another dimension, I was given a vision of an Indian holy man standing behind Daran. My heart skipped a beat as I recognized the holy man as Sri Yukteswar who had been Paramahansa Yogananda's guru in the early twentieth century. I had read Yogananda's *Autobiography of a Yogi* many years before and had wept with joy at his description of the poignant reunion with his guru in this lifetime.

Then in my mind's eye I could see the guru lovingly place his hands on Daran's shoulders. In the next moment he seemed to merge his being with Daran's, so that Daran's face was now Sri Yukteswar's face. The vision lasted only about 10 seconds and then dissolved. After the session I shared my vision with Daran, and he told me that while he was playing he had *felt it*—a powerful, loving presence merging with him. The energy of love coming into him had been so intense and joyful that he was overcome with emotion. He thought he might start to cry and not be able to continue playing. Not coincidentally, Daran told me that he had just started to read *Autobiography of a Yogi*! Nothing is random.

Separating Ourselves (Seemingly) from Love

The world is rife with examples of our having gotten lost in the predominant illusions of our cultures and of our having forgotten about love. As I've talked about before, based on the pervasive norm of glorifying competition and separateness in the world, much of humanity has bought into the illusion that people can be divided into categories such as us vs. them or winners vs. losers. The enduring constructs of nationalism and patriotism, for example, are built on the belief that the people of one's own nation are not only different from the people of other nations but are superior to them. Especially during these times of unending war we're encouraged to buy into the deception that some human beings are even inherently our sworn enemies. How else could we justify waging war on them? How else could we rationalize destroying their homes, their livelihoods, torturing them, and taking their lives?

We're able to wage war on our so-called enemies because on some level we believe that they are less than human. When people of different countries or political affiliations or religions are dehumanized and demonized, the aggressors can rationalize that those who are less than human do not deserve respect or humane treatment. The atrocities committed against them in war and at other times can then be deemed acceptable or even appropriate. In the ultimate reality that is spiritual reality there is no such thing as us and them, winners and losers, allies and enemies. We are all just *Spirit's beloveds.*

Another pervasive illusory belief is that happiness and being loved and accepted can be attained through amassing wealth and striving for social status. This mindset can create tremendous suffering for those who believe the premise. Often the suffering is caused by our fears that we're not good enough or cool enough if we don't own the latest model of some consumer item or if we don't look young and sexually attractive. Economies are fed by never ending advertising and media messages that encourage those fears.

The constant stream of fear messages keeps many of us in a state of emotional disequilibrium, always wanting something more in order to be content, guaranteeing that contentment is never reached. Sometimes these messages are subliminal, not accessible to the conscious mind, and sometimes they're quite blatant. In a society where most people are not yet awake, these messages are powerful motivators. A case in point is the common scene in the early morning hours of the day after Thanksgiving, a day when millions of Americans begin their holiday shopping. All over the country mobs of shoppers surge into stores, afraid that they won't be able to purchase the items that they believe they or their children need to be happy. The race into stores can be so frantic and full of anxiety that some shoppers and bystanders have been trampled and injured. Some have even been crushed to death. A quote I read once that comes from the book, *Empire of Illusion: The End of Literacy and the Triumph of Spectacle* by Pulitzer Prize-winning author, Chris Hedges, comes to mind: "A culture… which fails to understand that the measure of a civilization is its compassion, not its speed or ability to consume, condemns itself to death."[5]

While engendering much discord and fear, however, the drama created by buying into material illusions can be seductive, especially in a society where we're not encouraged to look beneath the surface of our lives. What's more, pressure to conform to the prevailing beliefs in one's group can be enormous, and refusing to do what is expected may elicit some dire consequences. The consequences of refusing to obey a group's norms can range from subtle pressure (as in asking a woman, "Aren't you planning to have children?" or asking a man, "What do you mean you don't like football"?) to outright ostracism. In some instances that pressure can be relentless and compelling. Around the world, even in this twenty-first century, people who are considered different and who don't submit to group control, who don't look and act like everyone else in the majority, are often considered malevolent and deviant. They can be ostracized and persecuted and sometimes even tortured and killed.

In 1967, Dr. Martin Luther King, Jr. delivered a powerful speech entitled, "Beyond Vietnam: A Time to Break Silence," in which he called for a revolution of values. He challenged us to embrace values that transcend the illusions of the world, like the belief that people are separate from each other. He challenged nations to develop an "all-embracing and unconditional love for all mankind," which he believed was needed for humanity's very *survival*,

> "When I speak of love I am not speaking of some sentimental and weak response. … I am speaking of that force which all of the great religions have seen as the supreme unifying principle of life. Love is somehow the key that unlocks the door which leads to ultimate reality."[6]

It's understandable that we've bought into the illusions of the material plane, however. There are forces in the world, driven by people who either remain ignorant of spiritual truth or who choose to live in darkness, who want us to believe that the illusions are reality. These are individuals who have identified with negative and dark forces, and who would like us to remain fear-bound in order to keep us under control. They want us to live in constant fear because fear keeps us out of our center, and when we're not centered we're not in touch with the love that we are or with the immense power of that love.

At this moment we are being challenged to actively participate in the material realm and to enjoy all it has to offer without getting hooked into the seeming reality generated by its illusions. We are being asked to look beyond the surface appearance of circumstances and events—especially when there is chaos and upheaval in those events. We are being reminded to go beneath the surface aspects of our experience to that spaciousness within of quiet and peace. It's there that we can feel and remember that the underlying reality, the underlying potential in all things, is always, always the energy and power of divine love.

Spirit is speaking to you now through me ...

*Dream with me, Dear One, until you remember the truth that endures beneath everything else: that **you are the greatest joy** of this Dreamer who dreamt the earth into ecstatic form. Dream with me now, Beloved, as you remember that you are starlight and moonlight and the infinite light of my heart. Remember with me that within your own glorious heart is the One Love that lies beneath the facade and illusions of all the manifest world.*

CHAPTER V

Compassion: The Art of Loving— Starting with Yourself

I have come into this world to see this:
the sword drop from men's hands
even at the height of their arc of rage
because we have finally realized
there is just one flesh we can wound

Hafiz[1]

The Experience and Power of Compassion: Starting With Yourself

Many years ago I was struggling with terrible regret and self-recrimination over something I'd done—actually something I had repeatedly wished on an old boyfriend. Teary-eyed and feeling ashamed, I asked Spirit, How on earth do you deal with someone like me? Someone who should know better, someone who *does* know better? The response from the voice that speaks to me was, *"Very gently."* I cried out loud, feeling unworthy of the sweet compassion coming through those words. Closing my eyes I was soon shown hands of light gently stroking and smoothing out my energy field, and I started to calm down and feel comforted. *Very gently* is how Spirit comes to you as well, no matter what you've done.

Many of us can admit to having regrets or feelings of outright guilt over things we did or said—or failed to do or say. Even after many years we may still feel bad about the times we put our selfish desires over the real needs of someone else. We may still feel bad about our errors in judgment or the times when we were mean and petty or worse. But what if Spirit doesn't want us to drag around our heavy feelings of guilt year after year? What if we're really meant to see ourselves as unskillful or ignorant or unconscious instead of evil? What if we really understood that we're all just works in progress, each of us doing the best we can? Wouldn't that change everything?

The fact remains that until we're able to forgive ourselves, until we're able to have compassion for ourselves—just as we are—we will not be able to fully feel the love surrounding us. The love that is our very essence. Only when we've been able to give ourselves the gift of loving kindness, will we be able to know and truly feel that we are dearly loved.

Unfortunately, many of us have internalized the punitive parental voice from childhood, and it now seems to be our own. That punishing and hypercritical voice in your head, however, is not the voice of Spirit. Let me repeat, it's not the voice of Spirit. You and I need to take a risk and "detach with love," as Buddhism suggests, from the sound of that harsh inner voice.

Of course, compassion for ourselves is often easier said than done. Most cultures have a judgmental and unforgiving side, and they condition us to make constant disparaging pronouncements on ourselves and virtually everything that comes into our purview. I was programmed from childhood to judge everything and everyone, and not in any positive sense like being discerning in my choices or making observations about the world without adding value judgments. No, I unsympathetically made constant mental decrees on the value of virtually everything that came into my awareness. My evaluations were not all negative or critical, though. There were many people I could admire and like and respect, and there were people I felt love for. And I've rarely met an animal I didn't immediately love. But since I had secretly hated myself since childhood and had not yet begun to awaken, I learned to project my self-criticism out onto the world. Since I had been shamed so much growing up, I vacillated between, on the one hand, unconsciously projecting my shame and judgments onto others, thus making them bad or wrong, and on the other, feeling my shame so acutely that I felt I didn't deserve to take up space in the world.

As I began to practice mindfulness, though, I could see that my constant judging used up a lot of mental energy and kept me in a kind of prison. Releasing myself from this prison entailed releasing the need to endlessly evaluate others and myself. As I became more mindful I discovered that I could give myself permission to just feel what I felt and experience what I experienced without having to analyze it all.

By suspending our habitual, disapproving judgments we also allow ourselves the freedom to be open to alternate realities that may exist just beyond our critical verdicts. For example, if we're mindful, we're focused on what is right here and right now; the individual we judged to be one way a year ago or a minute ago may not be the same in this present moment. Many times I have approached someone with only my past interactions with them in mind, and been surprised that they'd moved on while I was still dragging the past with me. In the same way, wouldn't it be lovely if others with whom we have past history could come to us as we are now, in the present? If we could lessen our grip on this lens of criticism through which we view ourselves and the world we would just be free.

That being said, even at this point in my life, disparaging thoughts still seem to arise all on their own. When I'm paying attention I can gently remind myself that I don't need to judge anyone or anything anymore, including myself. I can observe the critical thoughts without needing to judge even the fact that they've arisen, and then I can let them go. But I understand that for some of us, forgiving ourselves after we've made serious mistakes can be an act of absolute daring. I know full well that it can take an act of blind faith to trust in our inherent goodness when we're confused and unsure and down on ourselves.

Every now and then a memory of something I did or didn't do will be triggered by some seemingly random event and I'll feel an old, painful pang of guilt or sadness. I used to do anything I could to resist these memories, but now I see them and the wincing pain they elicit as my teachers, messengers of where I'm lacking in self-compassion. Now I'll allow myself to feel the discomfort of the memory while I call in what's commonly referred to as the witness mind. The witness mind just observes whatever is arising in consciousness without needing to evaluate anything as noble or evil. From the witness vantage point I try to understand what I'd been afraid of, what I'd been hurting over, that could have led me to do or say what I now regret. Just trying to understand the fear and pain behind my less than perfect behavior helps me to begin to soften.

Sometimes I'll say the prayer from the ancient Hawaiian shamanic practice for healing called Ho'oponopono, popularized in recent years by Dr. Hew Len and Dr. Joe Vitale. The prayer is, "I love you, I'm sorry." I'll recite the prayer in my heart to whomever I may have hurt, intentionally or unintentionally. I may also say it to myself in those countless situations where I didn't value and respect myself. I'll repeat the prayer as many times as I need to until I feel that a shift of my heart energy has occurred and I can feel the flow of compassion for myself. Then I can let go of the thoughts and the painful feeling of remorse in that moment. The more I say the prayer the more the old memories are cleared and released.

When we can muster the courage to give ourselves a little tenderness, something softens in us, and the willingness to offer understanding to other beings who are suffering begins to arise naturally. And it gets easier to come to ourselves with loving kindness as we come to the realization that we are fundamentally the same as everyone else who's ever struggled with their inner demons. In this regard, any consideration of compassion begins with this understanding: you and I want to be happy and all beings want to be happy. You and I want to love and be loved just as all beings want to love and be loved. You and I want to avoid suffering just as all beings want to avoid suffering. Ultimately, the practice of compassion begins with our desire to understand the root of this suffering, our own and another's. It's begins with the opening of our hearts to our own pain and confusion and then to another's as if it were our own. On the spiritual level—the level of our unseen, energetic connection to all beings—it *is* our own pain.

Life is Like a School

Life is like a school. Some "students" are further along on the path of enlightenment (have experienced more and learned or remembered more) than others. Just as we don't expect a first grader to understand calculus, we don't expect some souls to understand the deeper reality of life at their particular level of unfolding. Ultimately, however, we will all complete the course; we will all come to realize the spiritual truth about life.

Choosing the response of compassion implies not condemning the behavior of someone and not making judgments about their worth. Each and every soul has the same inherent worth as part of Spirit, and yet life lessons and soul purpose can be different for each of us. How can we judge another's behavior since we can never truly know the path another soul is on? How can we ever truly know the suffering that someone else has been through? But when we can access the well of compassion within ourselves, we can acknowledge that if we had lived the life of that person whose actions or feelings seem foreign or unforgivable to us, we might very well be feeling the same feelings and behaving in the same way that they are. And isn't it true that most of us have had the experience of criticizing someone else's behavior and then realizing, with some chagrin, that we, ourselves, have engaged in that very behavior at one time or another.

There's a well-known Native American saying (purportedly from the Cheyenne) that relates to this: "Do not judge your neighbor until you walk two moons in his moccasins." The two moons are actually two moon cycles of 28 days. So the adage is asking us to live a person's life for two months before we presume to pass judgment. Please know, however, that a compassionate opening of your heart to another's pain and suffering does not nullify that person's responsibility for his or her behavior. Each of us is responsible for our choices and our actions, but responsibility does not equal blame. There is still no one to blame. What compassion means is that when someone (like us) behaves badly, when they (we) hurt other beings, they (we) have gotten stuck in some kind of pain and fear of loss. That fear could be over the loss of love or loss of control, loss of material security or status, or loss of affiliation. They—we—have gotten lost temporarily, but at some point in our soul's evolving, each of us will eventually make our way back to the empathy and understanding that engenders compassion.

Just as our choosing compassion for ourselves or another doesn't negate our personal accountability, neither does it mean that we cannot draw some boundaries with another. But we're still meant to hold that person in our heart without hatred and without a sense of being separate from him or her. We're still meant to keep our heart open to that individual's pain. Ultimately it is our pain as well.

We also have the choice of reframing our life situations within the much larger context of reincarnation and the soul's choices. In that regard, people who've been hypnotically regressed back to the time between lifetimes, often speak of making agreements or "sacred contracts" with members of their soul group about the upcoming lifetime. All agreements and plans are decided on in absolute love, with the goal of helping each other evolve by means of providing the challenges that allow us to deepen our compassion. Even when the life events that are planned don't seem very loving, they are conceived of from a place of love. For instance, if a man betrays his partner in a previous lifetime and feels no compassion or remorse, his partner might agree, out of a higher love, to betray him in the next lifetime. In this way his partner is giving him the opportunity to learn how painful the experience of betrayal can be so that he can deepen his capacity for empathy and compassion. All of our life crises are ultimately about healing. They offer us the opportunity to heal and evolve, and we have co-created them out of a higher love.

The details of the contracts we make with other souls are not written in stone, however; they may be thought of as a kind of flexible blueprint of potential and probability. When the upcoming lifetime is experienced, the agreed upon plans may or may not need to come to fruition because other life experiences, as well as our willingness to heal, may have already provided us with the opportunities to learn compassion.

Inevitably, one day each of us will understand that the hurt we've caused others and ourselves has been a direct outcome of our being caught in our fears. This understanding may not happen in this lifetime, but it will happen. As beings of light we are meant to heal, and that healing will invariably involve our waking up to the things we could have done better, that is, with greater awareness and compassion. We will then feel and understand the effects of our less-than-mindful thoughts and actions. At that time we must remind ourselves that we are worthy of understanding and compassion as well.

Please remember, you are dearly loved just as you are. There's no need to reject any part of yourself or of anyone else. If we can have a little gentle understanding for those things within ourselves that we're afraid to see and feel, we can heal our sense of separation from the rest of life, and that is a profound healing.

All of Life is a Continuum

The individuality and separateness of people is real in the world of form. In the manifest world we interact with other people and have relationships with them. We can be challenged by others and have great love with them. Cultivating our distinct individuality can even be considered an act of service to the world as well as to ourselves. No one else in the world has your unique, matchless gifts to give.

But if we are all individualized expressions of one divine love, then there is no true *spiritual* "other." There is no creature on the earth (or anywhere in the universe) who is completely separate energetically from us. Albert Einstein has been quoted in many places as saying that our belief in the complete separateness of people is,

> "a kind of prison for us, restricting us to our personal desires and to affection for a few persons nearest us. Our task must be to free ourselves from this prison by widening our circle of compassion to embrace all living creatures and the whole of nature in its beauty."[2]

A major step in widening our circle of compassion occurs when we can see a part of ourselves in another and can see another in ourselves. When we can see another as someone with the same fear as ours of not being good enough, the same desire as ours to be happy, and the same fear of hurt and suffering, we've gone a long way in our emotional and spiritual evolution. Many traditions have embraced this concept. In Cherokee teachings, for example, there's a principle that is an integral part of their wisdom: whenever we feel that we're different from someone else, we are to remember our shared humanity with the statement, "That in him or her is like this in me." And when Hindus and Buddhists and others use the greeting, "Namasté," its meaning is based on the concept of the unity of all souls. This Sanskrit word can be translated, "I honor the divine in you which is also in me." The extended meaning of the term continues, "When you are in that (divine) place within yourself and I am in that place within myself, we are One."

I understand that it may be difficult to feel connected to all other beings and to know that a part of them is a part of you. It may be especially difficult when you don't want to be connected to someone—when you don't like what they do or say or how they interpret the world. Perhaps you recognize something of yourself in them and you don't like what you see. For instance, you may feel an aversion to the angry and aggressive behavior of another because deep down you're really afraid of feeling and perhaps acting on your own angry impulses. This leads us to consideration of what Carl Jung referred to as our "shadow."

Our Shadow

One does not become enlightened by imagining figures of light but by making the darkness conscious. Carl Jung[3]

Before I started to become conscious I often did whatever I could to avoid the company of people who demanded to be the center of attention and who never stopped talking. When I finally decided to do some introspecting and pay loving attention to those feelings within me, I began to wonder where my intense resistance was coming from. With the willingness to be honest with myself, I came to realize that I was afraid to let myself see and feel my own need (at that time in my life) to control everyone's attention. I began to realize that all of us have the capacity to deny a dark part of ourselves, a part that frightens us—our own "shadow." In effect, we disown it. So in rejecting another, we're actually rejecting a part of ourselves.

What if the shadow side of us were not truly a dark part? What if those thoughts and feelings and impulses are only considered dark because they're hidden to our conscious mind and because we're afraid of claiming them as a part of ourselves? In *Heal Thy Self*, Dr. Saki Santorelli speaks of the need to enter the terrifying "realm of our broken and unwanted places"[4] in order to heal. He discusses a theme in Western fairy tales and myths that refers to the unexpected benefits, the "gold" as it were, of doing the inner work of facing those unwanted places. First it's necessary to uncover what we have denied in ourselves so that we can see our own capacity for such things as self-deception and deceit, and our own greed and grief and shame. If we choose to not face what we have disowned, however, "we remain blind, unconsciously driven by these unattended-to forces."[5]

Once we can face our unenlightened selves with a sense of curiosity instead of self-condemnation, we will inevitably experience a "death of much of what we have imagined ourselves to be,"[6] that is, we'll come to know that the lower selves of our egos and their masks don't define us. With that "death" we'll be led to the insight that we are not those capabilities or qualities of our shadow. We'll have discovered the hidden treasure that lies at the end of this process: the awareness of who we really are, the pure consciousness and goodness underneath it all. In my experience, when I've been able to go into and through my woundedness and ignorance, my inner darkness, with a kind of detached gentleness, I have ultimately come to the gold of knowing my inner light as well. Transpersonal psychologist, John Welwood, expresses so well what I have experienced:

> "You are flawed, you are stuck in old patterns, you become carried away with yourself. Indeed you are quite impossible in many ways. And still, you are beautiful beyond measure. For the core of what you are is fashioned out of love, that potent blend of openness, warmth, and clear, transparent presence."[7]

By doing the shadow work with a sense of just noticing what is, without self-criticism, we come to the deep understanding that we are not our thoughts and we are not our emotions. They are ephemera—they change and flow all the time. Sometimes they seem to arise out of nowhere and then recede. There is nothing permanent about them. Thoughts and feelings and impulses are just forms of energy that flow through us; they are not our essence. When we can see that we humans are, at heart, all the same, with the same struggle to awaken and to make conscious that which is still hidden, we can soften to ourselves and our own suffering, and then soften into compassion for all beings who suffer.

I'm reminded of a presentation I attended years ago at a New Life Expo in New York City. It was given by Dr. Elizabeth Kübler-Ross, the noted Swiss-American psychiatrist. She was probably most famous for her research and writing about death and dying, having introduced the concept of the five stages of grief. The opening words of her talk were in the form of a shocking question. "How many of you sitting here have a Hitler inside you?" she asked.

There was bewildered silence in the large audience as we tried to process what she meant. Was she really asking if any of us thought we were sociopaths who were capable of perpetrating genocide on a massive scale? I didn't think that was what she was asking. I interpreted her question to mean how many of us believed that we had the capacity to feel irrational hatred and could be capable, perhaps, of murderous violence. There were only a few of us who began to raise our hands in acknowledgment of our own potential dark side, but as I looked around at the rest of the audience with their hands in their laps, I quickly put my hand down. Dr. Kübler-Ross's next words were stunning: "You all have a Hitler in you." Some in attendance seemed to be shocked by her declaration, but I knew that she was trying to help us understand that we were not completely separate from *anyone*. All expressions of violence exist on a continuum; we can commit an act of emotional violence by using our words to inflict hurt or we can physically assault someone. Ultimately, given the right circumstances, we all have the same capacity for the whole range of human feeling and behavior.

Caring about others who are displaying emotions or behaviors that we don't like or that we resist in some way entails having the strength to face the fear and pain of finding those emotions or behaviors in ourselves. When we can do that, it's the beginning of genuine compassion. Eminent Buddhist teacher, Pema Chödrön, has suggested,

> "Compassion is not a relationship between the healer and the wounded. It's a relationship between equals. Only when we know our own darkness well can we be present with the darkness of others. Compassion becomes real when we recognize our shared humanity."[8]

If it seems too difficult right now to imagine yourself ever feeling or acting the way another feels or acts, perhaps you have not yet been tested by life in the same way that they have. Perhaps you have different life lessons. I do understand that being able to feel a connection to and have compassion for someone who has hurt you can be very challenging especially when their suffering is not obvious. I offer you that they may be afraid to show their vulnerability by admitting they're in pain, even to themselves. But it's an act of love to even try to understand another through their suffering, If we take the time to explore what underlies their behavior, what is the root of their pain, we'll see where they hurt, and compassion will begin to arise. In that vein, Ram Dass and Paul Gorman, in their amazing *How Can I Help? Stories and Reflections on Service,* have written about quieting our mind and listening deeply so that we,

> "can reach out and hear, as from inside, the heart of someone's pain. Each time we are able to remain open to suffering, despite our fear and defensiveness, we sense a love in us which becomes increasingly unconditional."[9]

It remains for all of us that underneath our "crimes" or misdeeds where we have hurt life in some way, we are still just infinite consciousness, infinite goodness, here on earth to experience and remember the beauty of love. I read the following quote once from the great poet and artist, William Blake, whose beautiful lines capture this sentiment:

And we are put on earth a little space
That we might learn to bear the beams of love.

A Gift of Compassion: Richard Pryor

Many years ago Spirit gave me my first major lesson in the utter joy that compassion can generate. It was 1980 when Richard Pryor made the news for having set himself on fire. A well-known comedian and actor, he had a reputation for being edgy and iconoclastic. I had only been engaged in my spiritual and psychic awakening for a short time then, and I was still stuck in feeling different from most people. I felt inferior to most, superior to some, and Richard Pryor was not one of my favorite celebrities. In my profound ignorance, I felt totally separate from him.

When I heard what had happened to him, though, it was as if I had been struck by lightning. Someone or something unseen said to me, "Sit down and pray for Richard." I was not really into praying in those days, but I did begin to pray intently. I prayed for whatever power of healing that may have existed to help Richard survive and heal. I can't tell you how I was able to feel this but somehow I could feel that my good wishes were part of a great wave of love and healing energy being sent to him.

As I prayed he came into my mind and I saw him sitting still with his hands on his knees and his head facing upward. He seemed to be trying to separate himself from the pain of his burns in order to survive. All of a sudden there was a feeling of having my energy shifted and I had no control over what was happening. It felt as if someone was lifting my disdain for Richard right out of my body. In the blink of an eye I was now able to empathize with him and his pain. I was able to feel how emotionally fragile and vulnerable he was beneath his facade. Instead of feeling completely separate from him, I was transformed with an overwhelming, compassionate love for him. I was astonished, and I just sat there for a short while, wondering where this grace was coming from.

I was then shown what I believed to be his soul, and it seemed to be absolutely pure and innocent. In my experience of the essence within him, there was no sense of the "score keeping" that I had expected, given my religious background, as in "Score one for God, one for Richard" kind of thing. What I perceived to be his soul seemed to be blameless and uncorrupted. It was a deep relief to be freed from those feelings of judgment and separation; they had simply been lifted from me. The whole experience was a gift, *a gift of compassion* from Spirit. I was filled with love for him then and I always will be.

There were some other interesting details of this vision that I was given. For instance, in my mind's eye I was shown something within Richard's chest and was told it was the bronchus. It was open and clear at the top but closed and twisted from scar tissue at the bottom, between the lungs. The voice that was speaking to me instructed me to put all the tissue and organs of his chest in healing light, which I did. I was then shown Richard's kidneys and was given the feeling that they were in shock and starting to fail. I was told to speak to them to reassure them that they were all right. So I imagined that I was gently stroking his kidneys to help calm them down, and I whispered to them that everything was okay and that they didn't have to panic.

At the time I was not aware of the fact that kidney failure is common in people with severe burns. Neither had I read anything about the fact that all of life had consciousness that could be communicated with. But intuitively it felt right to offer comfort and reassurance to Richard's kidneys and to send healing light to his organs.

In the years since my experience communicating with the consciousness of Richard's physical form, there's been a growing body of evidence-based research on the biochemical reality of the mind/body connection. (It's probably more accurate to view it as mind and spirit expressing as body, and I believe that someday there will be hard evidence for this.) It continues to be revealed that our neurological system communicates with our immune system and that these two systems interact with our endocrine system, all with the underpinning of and interaction with our emotions.

Research pioneers like the late Dr. Candace Pert and her colleagues at Johns Hopkins and National Institutes of Mental Health were able to find material evidence of this interaction between our emotions and our biochemistry. Dr. Pert's book, *Molecules of Emotion: The Science Behind Mind-Body Medicine*, is a fascinating description of her process of discovery. All living things have consciousness, including the cells of our bodies. If we are experiencing happiness or anxiety or sadness, as we believe can now be measured by certain molecules and their receptor sites on cell membranes, then apparently all of our cells are registering happiness, anxiety, or sadness as well.

As I continued to pray for Richard, I knew somehow that what I was about to witness was taking place in the so-called future. I could see the skin grafts that were to be performed on him in the days ahead. I could see pink skin being grafted onto his burn sites. When I mentioned to a friend that this vision couldn't be accurate because the grafts weren't the color of his unburned skin, he reminded me that skin grafts are taken from the underlying layer of skin. That layer is pink in all of us, regardless of the color of the epidermis.

I refer to the future as "so-called" because, as I understand it, the constructs of time and space are illusions. When we raise our vibration to a higher state of consciousness, the fact that we're able to perceive events at a great distance or in another time period is an indication that all of existence is part of a single unified energetic field. Time and space only appear to exist; they're a kind of artifact imposed on our perception of reality. If we refocus our consciousness in such a way as to access the unified field's information, those artificial structures of space and time disappear. Tuning in to Richard's energy, I was apparently able to access the level of the unified field, the Universal Mind, where there is neither physical nor temporal distance between us.

Peering into the future again, I could see and hear his doctors talking about how miraculous his healing was. Later I read somewhere that his healing was indeed considered a miracle. I also read that when Richard was first admitted to the hospital, he had the feeling of actually being lifted off his hospital bed from the strength of all the prayers coming to him. I was filled with gratitude that so many of us were sending love to him and that he was able to feel it. And I was grateful to be reminded on a deep level that love is a force, it is real, and it has the power to create miracles.

Years later I was able to see this same process played out through another scenario. After her death, my father's sister communicated to me through a medium that when she left her body and crossed over into Spirit, her animosity toward my mother was lifted from her and was replaced with love. I believe that my experience of being given the feeling of love and connection with Richard was a little taste of that heavenly release and transformation.

From this gift of compassion I received I learned that I can't ever get away with seeing another being as totally separate from myself—no matter who they are or what they do. Neither can I condemn nor make judgments about what they're going through or what their scorecard is with Spirit. Of course, when I'm in "automatic pilot" mode, that is, when I'm not being mindful, it is only too easy to slip back into the old, erroneous way of thinking. I experience this slipping into mindlessness fairly often, and I've come to realize that there's no way I know of to prevent a judgmental thought or feeling from arising. The key is to do my best to be aware of what I'm giving attention to in the moment. When I can be conscious of where my mind has gone, I can release my critical thoughts and reaffirm the other's true nature as well as my own. I can then choose to refrain from acting out of ego/fear-based judgments.

As I have said before, even if you don't remember why you chose this path, to Spirit you are a hero just for having come to this planet with great bravery and the highest form of love. You are the hero who, in your deepest and perhaps forgotten self, has compassion for the pain and suffering of all beings and wants to help all beings heal. Even if you don't remember, you know that until all beings have recognized their true identity and have freed themselves from their fear and limiting beliefs, neither you nor I are truly free.

The voice of Spirit is whispering to you now...

Dear One, once you have felt the deep relief of knowing that you are goodness itself—as Spirit in form—you will know that you are worthy of love. You will no longer be afraid to soften.... and let compassion flow. Once you have understood how inexpressibly beautiful you are to Spirit, you will no longer be afraid to go within to access a tender understanding for your own suffering.

Beloved, this Great Spirit of All That Is and All That Can Be is whispering to you—that you are and always will be my unending and boundless joy. As you allow this to be true, your loving kindness will start to flow, first for yourself. Then it will radiate out from you like gentle rain falling on a parched countryside, with all the thirsty beings soaking it up as if they'd never been loved before. You and I will thus take this living earth and all her precious beings into the arms of our gentle understanding, and we'll whisper to all who are suffering now: We're holding you close in our hearts as we bathe you all in the sweetest and softest rain of comfort and grace and love.

May all beings know their utter and infinite goodness. May all beings know that they are worthy of love and that they're being held in the arms of Spirit's love as if they were cherished children. May all who have life know that they are, indeed, dearly loved.

Tonglen, a Buddhist Meditative Practice on Compassion

Tonglen is a Tibetan word that means "giving and receiving" or "sending and receiving." It involves our taking in the suffering we see and feel around us (the receiving) and giving back our loving kindness and tenderness (the giving), and we do this through the medium of the breath. Through our inhalation we take on the pain and negativity of others and through our exhalation we send back peace and calm. We can do the taking in of pain and the giving back of love and comfort with our breath as long as we wish and wherever we see or know that people or animals are suffering.

The Practice

You begin Tonglen by calming your mind and centering yourself as best you can. Then,

- Attuning your awareness to another's suffering, you imagine breathing it all into yourself. You take it in and absorb it as if you are lifting the burden of pain from the suffering individual. Breathing in slowly, while picturing the person who is suffering, you say, "I breathe in your pain" (or confusion or fear or whatever).
- Breathing out, you send your peace or Spirit's peace or comfort to the person in pain. Slowly exhaling you say, "I breathe out my peace to you."

This practice will help you tap into a wellspring of loving kindness within yourself. I like to end this exercise with the affirmations: May I be well. May I be happy. May all beings be well. May all beings be happy.

If you feel empty and unable to access compassion for another, you can use Tonglen to access it first for yourself, although that's often more difficult. An exercise for doing Tonglen for yourself follows as well as a Tonglen practice to unblock your heart's energies.

Tonglen for Yourself

Many of us have difficulty releasing feelings of regret or guilt, but using Tonglen for ourselves can help us to do that. The following version of Tonglen may help you to deepen and strengthen your capacity for self-love and compassion.

- You begin by imagining a division of yourself into two parts. One part is imagined to be the nonjudgmental part of you— the part of you that is already healed and has compassion for yourself and all your suffering, It's often referred to as Part A.
- The other part, Part B, is the part of you that is hurting.
- Your Part A self then opens his or her heart with the sincere wish to alleviate the suffering of your Part B self and draws in, on the inhalation, Part B's hurt and negativity and fear.
- With as much compassionate understanding as you can manage, as you exhale, Part A sends your hurting self peace and comfort and healing love.

Tonglen for Unblocking Your Heart's Energies

If you're feeling emotionally blocked, there's a Tonglen technique that can help you unblock your heart's energies. The practice begins with bringing someone to mind who has touched you with their love for you.

- Allowing yourself to remember the feeling of being loved by them, you let that memory elicit a feeling of gratitude toward them.

- You then imagine this gratitude deepening and flowing into love, and you send that love out to the person who has loved you.
- Lastly you imagine extending this love out to those you know well, then to those you are acquainted with, then to those you've never met, and finally to all beings.

May all beings know that they are dearly loved.

In Tonglen, the sender benefits as much as the receiver does. When we take in others' pain and send out our love and peace to them, over time we begin to feel that love and peace for ourselves. Feeling the relief of love for ourselves, we begin to remember with joy our own basic goodness and the basic goodness of all other beings. As Sogyal Rinpoche has written in *Tibetan Book of Living and Dying*, "all are blessed and healed" in Tonglen and,

> "... whoever prompts you to develop compassion by their suffering is in fact giving you one of the greatest gifts of all, because they are helping you to develop that very quality you need most in your progress toward enlightenment."[10]

I do Tonglen on a regular basis since it appears that there's a seemingly infinite supply of pain and suffering in the world—both in the outside world and within my own internal world. Once in a while, tuning in to and feeling the suffering can be absolutely overwhelming. When that happens I want to erupt with a primal scream that comes from the bottom of my being for all the harm that is done by us, and for the ensuing pain. Then I remind myself that love in the form of compassion is the most powerful and miraculous force on earth. It's more powerful than fear or guilt or rage or hatred, even though these emotions may seem to be powerful in the moment. Love in the form of compassion is powerful enough to alleviate our suffering and wipe our karmic slates clean. Only compassion can connect us with our authentic self, our essential goodness, which lies beyond the mind. Only the choice of open-hearted compassion as a response to inner pain or external conflict can ever bring us genuine peace. Only compassion.

CHAPTER VI

All Beings Are Dearly Loved

Start seeing everything as God
But keep it a secret.

Become like the man who is Awestruck
And Nourished

Listening to a Golden Nightingale
Sing in a beautiful foreign language
While God invisibly nests
Upon its tongue.

Hafiz[1]

Compassion for All Beings

One day the absurdity of the almost universal human belief in the slavery of other animals will be palpable. We shall then have discovered our souls and become worthier of sharing this planet with them. (Attributed to Dr. Martin Luther King, Jr.)

When I suggest that all beings are loved and worthy of compassion I am referring not only to human beings but to all nonhuman animals as well. This includes birds and fish and marine mammals and reptiles and any sentient being. They deserve kindness and compassion as well as any human being does since all of life is the energy of divine love in form.

Animals are my heart. I was born loving them, revering them, as if it were hard wired in me. There's something magical and higher order about them. I can't imagine a world without animals and birds and all the other amazing creatures who share this planet with us. I wouldn't want to live in a world without them. Anyone who has ever loved a dog or a cat, a horse or a bird, an elephant or a lion or any creature knows how much sheer joy they bring us. For many of us there is something so primal in our attraction to the animals who grace our lives and our planet that it's close to impossible to give words to the love and gratitude we feel for them. I'm also hard-wired to be of service to my nonhuman sisters and brothers as well as to my human ones. I've rescued dogs and cats and wounded birds. I've put worms gently back in the grass after a heavy rain has deposited them in the street, and I've gotten out of the car to move a turtle from the middle of the road. I've stood on many a protest line as well to demand justice for animals and marine mammals.

I believe that all the nonhuman beings who are with us are here out of a higher love, from which they help us to balance our personal energy as well as help to balance the energies of the earth with their beauty. They help us to be even more human, since their unconditional presence and love opens our hearts, and we are more like our true selves when we are open-hearted. I've come to realize that in their openness and innocence, animals remind us of our own basic goodness and innocence, and that is a grand and glorious gift.

For as long as I can remember whenever I've entered a room with an animal in it, my attention is immediately drawn to the animal no matter how many people are there. It's like there's a spiritual magnet pulling me toward the consciousness and heart of the animal. My father used to tell me that even as a toddler I would rush to the side of a stray or tied up dog. He would try to restrain me or caution me about petting the animal but nothing could stop me. He'd hold his breath until he saw the dog do a soft tail wag or in some way show that he wouldn't be aggressive. I had also begged him for a tiger when I was little, assuring him that we could keep the tiger in our garage and that I would take care of him. Of course as a child I didn't realize that confining a wild animal to a small space would constitute abuse.

I have often asked clients and friends "What would you do if you had no fear?" When I ask myself that question, I fantasize telling everyone I meet that I loved them (liking them might be a different story!). I don't have the nerve to do that just yet, but I show people that I love them by giving them my attention and respect. On the other hand I don't fear being ridiculed or considered crazy by all the dogs and cats I openly profess my love to! Some people do give me strange looks, though, when they overhear me repeatedly whispering to the resident parrot where I work that she's beautiful and that I love her and that I'm so sorry she's stuck in that cage by herself. She seems to soak up the love. She coos with my words and the sound of my voice and inevitably her eyes begin to close and she drifts off to sleep. The unabashed delight I feel from this connection makes up for any suspicion I might get from bystanders. (If staff member, Kevin, is around, however, all bets are off. She only has eyes for him.)

I offer you this premise: when we take the time and make the effort to pay attention to the energy of the animals around us we begin to realize that they are individuals with unique personalities and needs and feelings. They are worthy of our respect and protection. The biblical phrase "dominion over the animals" does not mean our domination or exploitation of them. It does not mean that we have the right to use them for entertainment or profit or kill them for what is outrageously called trophies. What it does mean is that we're given the sacred responsibility of being their stewards, their guardians, entrusted with keeping them safe from human harm and interference as well as protecting their habitats and the world's ecosystems.

There are some images you just can't get out of your mind once you've seen them. They haunt you. One of these shocking and heartbreaking images for me is of men clubbing baby seals to death in front of their mothers in order to harvest their fur. If the babies were human, we'd know the agony of their mothers who have to witness this barbarism. We'd also arrest the murderers. But because the seals are "only animals," we don't. Let me assure you that I am no saint and have no wish to martyr myself, but each year since learning of this massacre, I have asked Spirit to help me find the wherewithal to get to the icy killing grounds so that I can put myself between the babies and the killers. I haven't been able to accomplish this yet, but when I do I will say to these men, "Club *me* to death, not these innocents." I would say the same thing to those who slaughter dolphins in Tajii, to the matadors who torture and kill bulls, to the poachers who are bringing elephants to the brink of extinction for their ivory tusks, to the majority of factory farmers around the world who give no thought to the misery of their animals and birds, to those in Asia who torture and kill dogs for their meat, and to all those who believe that we are not responsible for the suffering of nonhuman beings.

Animal Personhood

Animals have been considered chattel in all of recorded history. Their abuse and exploitation is not always illegal, but it is always unethical and inhumane. There is an ever-growing awareness, however, of how animals are suffering at the hands of humans. For one thing, it's becoming more common to refer to caretakers of animals not as owners but as guardians, acknowledging that they are not possessions but sentient beings worthy of protection. In that vein there's an organization called The Nonhuman Rights Project (NhRP²) that is pioneering in the use of common law and education to have animals granted the legal status of "persons." In this context the word person does not mean that animals are people but rather that they are unique individuals who have consciousness, who can feel pain and fear, and who are neither objects nor commodities.

NhRP litigates for personhood on behalf of some of the most intelligent animals like chimpanzees, elephants, and dolphins. Intelligence can be difficult to define and measure, and of course it's not the only criterion by which to judge the sanctity of animal life. The organization also speaks of the complexity of animal societies, their sophisticated communications, their use of tools for problem solving, and their capacity to mourn the loss of those close to them. But because our culture puts a premium on intellect as opposed to a more balanced, heart-centered way of being, perhaps litigating first for the rights of more intelligent animals will make it easier for people to identify with them. Maybe then it will seem less radical to accept the concept of their personhood. In any event, NhRP works toward securing the right of bodily liberty for wild animals, that is, to not be held in captivity, and the right of bodily integrity, to not be tortured or killed as part of such things as emergency medical training, biomedical research, or religious or secular "festivals."

Questions inevitably arise about the justification of using animals for food if indeed animals have the right of bodily integrity. Many of us feel that a vegan diet is the most ethical and sustainable one not only for the environmental health of the earth but for the soul of the human race. Until that is embraced by all people, we need to do our best to ensure that animals who are raised for food are not subjected to abuse and are treated humanely. It would also benefit us to thank and honor and bless the life of whatever we do consume.

Questions arise as well about our need to do scientific research on animals to find cures for human disease. A few things come to mind about this. First, many animal models do not translate well to human models. As I understand it, the use of live animals in emergency medicine training is outdated since there are excellent, high-tech human simulation models widely available. (See for example, Physicians Committee for Responsible Medicine[3] and American Anti-Vivisection Society (AAVS[4]). Secondly, for all of the legitimate research and experimentation that is done for the betterment of humanity, there are untold numbers of cruel and wasteful studies where animals are tortured and killed for utterly frivolous and worthless outcomes. (See, for example, White Coat Waste[5] and AAVS.) Lastly, it is my belief that once humanity truly values and honors the sanctity of life in all beings and in all forms, once all of us understand that no species is superior or more worthy of existence than another, we will have raised our vibration to such a high level that we will be spiritually transformed. At that level we will no longer be plagued by disease or famine or any other imbalance which we humans are prone to.

Communicating with Animal Persons

I have been communicating with the consciousness of animals for a long time, and their personhood is undeniable to me. I especially loved to connect with the horses of a dear friend of mine, Lightworker and artist Cindy McWilliams, who had a horse farm called "Bright Horse." Situated on breathtakingly beautiful land in Chatham County, North Carolina, Bright Horse combined art and equestrian education for children of all ages. Once while standing alone on the soil, I closed my eyes and breathed in the peace of the land. Before long a vision began to form in my mind of a powerful Native American looking into my eyes. He communicated to me that he had once lived on the land and considered it sacred as we did.

Of course I adored the horses. They were absolutely gorgeous and aware beings. Two of them, Debi and Zoë, were my favorites, and they bonded with me as we exchanged heart energy. Debi was a sensitive soul who would go to be with any horse who wasn't well even if they weren't normally friendly. She and I would play a game where she'd present her nose to me to be kissed.

I'd kiss, kiss, kiss while making a smooching sound and then turn my head to the right for a few seconds. She would turn her head away as well, except she turned to her left in order to mirror my action. Then she'd turn back toward me, presenting her face to be kissed again. We did this over and over. It was inexpressible joy.

Debi and Sheila
Photograph by Allen E. Shifrin

One day Cindy asked if I would communicate with Debi to ask her if she wanted to be a show horse for Cindy's two daughters. Debi said Absolutely Not. She was not comfortable competing. Her last guardians had tried to make her race and she wouldn't do it.

When I conveyed Debi's sentiments to Cindy she told me that the information helped her to understand a recent incident. Debi was an excellent jumper, but the last time she was taking Debi through her paces to assess her suitability for being a competitive jumper, Debi stopped mid-jump and Cindy went flying over her head. We surmised that Debi was communicating her great displeasure at the possibility of having to compete. Of course Cindy respected Debi's wishes. It was the most compassionate decision—and also the safest!

Every now and then Cindy asked me to communicate with one of the other horses in order to facilitate their healing. The first time was with gentle Zoë. Cindy asked me to visit Zoë to find out what was bothering her, apart from an injured leg that I knew about that had resulted from one of her frequent accidents. I didn't ask for details about her condition, and for some reason I just assumed that she had an illness. I met Zoë the next day, and speaking quietly to her I got her permission to enter her stall. She had the most beautiful, soft and soulful eyes and I was just drawn into her heart energy.

As I closed my eyes and tuned in to her consciousness I could feel a great sadness. I asked her why she was sad and she told me that she wasn't ill—she was mourning not having any babies. She was afraid that she never would. I stroked her neck and told her how sorry I was for her sadness. "I'm so sorry," I said. I just held her and loved her and acknowledged her pain. I know that she appreciated being seen—recognized as a unique and valued individual and as someone who had experiences and feelings. In a few minutes the message that came through for her was that if she didn't have babies of her own, there would be other foals and other beings around her who could really use her beautiful, nurturing love. I suggested this to her and I felt her energy begin to shift and lighten. Cindy told me later that even with veterinary care, a hormonal imbalance had prevented Zoë from maintaining her pregnancies. She'd had a series of miscarriages, the most recent one being a near-term stillbirth.

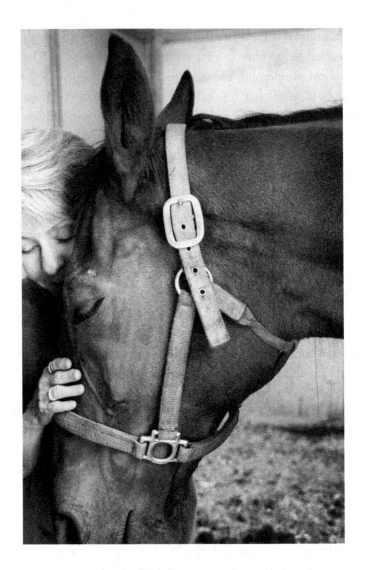

Zoë and Sheila
Photograph by Allen E. Shifrin

Also during that visit, with Zoë's permission, I placed my hands on her injured leg and asked Spirit to let its healing light flow through me to her. Cindy and the other Bright Horse artist had done this as well, and within a few days Zoë was walking easily again and was seemingly back to her healthy, happy self. As far as I knew, she had no more accidents. Her healing was a testament to the immense power of simple compassion.

Another of the horses was a magnificent, black beauty named Tara. She carried herself with even more stateliness and nobility than the others, and we regarded her affectionately as The Queen. One day Cindy called to tell me that Tara needed help. She'd been stall-bound for quite some time with one bone pressing on another in her right front lower leg, and this was causing her excruciating pain. The vet said that there was no surgery or other substantial treatment for the condition, and the only care was to try to ease her pain with potent analgesics. She was near the point of needing to be euthanized, and Cindy asked if I would tune in to Tara's consciousness and ask her how we could help. I couldn't make it to the farm physically that day but my mind and heart were there in an instant.

When I focused my awareness on Tara and got her permission to communicate with her, the first feeling I picked up was her utter exhaustion. So I imagined embracing her with brilliant, healing light that she seemed to absorb into her being. The living light would help rebalance and replenish and heal whatever needed healing. I knew that the most loving and useful thing I could do would be to visualize her as already healed and whole again within the light. I could see other souls around her, giving her healing energy as well, including several Native Americans who had loved her in other lifetimes. As I continued to cover her in Spirit's light I spoke to her higher self, telling her how much we loved her, now and always.

After a short while Tara showed me the image of her running with great pleasure across the land she loved. The question crossed my mind about whether the image represented one of Tara's memories or one of her wishes. The next scene unfolding was of her prancing sideways, doing a dressage step across the pasture. I had never seen her do that before, and I assumed that it was her desire to express her joy at being able to move with abandon over the land. I did wonder, though, if Tara was showing me these pictures to indicate that she'd be crossing over soon, where she'd be completely free and able to run and move in any way she wanted.

When I described the images that Tara had given me to Cindy, she told me that she had actually once trained Tara to do that very dressage step. Under the circumstances we both felt that it was highly possible that the scenes represented the spiritual realm of the other side, and that perhaps Tara was preparing us for her death. We were sad to think of her leaving the earth but we didn't want her to suffer. Cindy intuitively made the decision to not euthanize Tara just yet, however, and she remained on stall rest for quite a while. We continued daily to imagine her being embraced by living light, already healed.

One evening I got an excited call from Cindy telling me that Tara's condition was improving and that she had recovered sufficiently to actually gallop across the pasture! What's more, as she was making her way back to the barn that evening she had performed the sideways dressage step that Cindy had taught her! We believe that Tara had given us a glimpse of her future with the pictures she had transmitted to me. Cindy and I were overjoyed and so grateful to all who had participated in sending love and healing energy to Tara.

A couple of years later I was aware that Cindy was preparing to sell Bright Horse, but I didn't know exactly when that would occur or what would happen to the horses. One morning while I was meditating, Debi appeared to me and said goodbye. I soon learned that the farm had been sold and that Debi and Zoë had been given together to a good (home) farm.

Spirit Animals

As Native Americans and other indigenous cultures know well, the spirits of animals can be our teachers and guides. They come to us in visions and dreams and in the physical world to share their "medicine" with us, their knowledge and their power. These animal spirits are not mythical; they are energetic beings who love us and support us in meeting the challenges of our spiritual journey while on earth.

I had a lovely encounter with a Spirit Animal (or Spirit Bird as it were) as I was writing this chapter. One sun-filled afternoon I walked to the public garden near my home that overlooks the magnificent Hudson River. I'd wanted to read and write as I soaked up the serenity of the natural environment. As I entered the garden I heard the beautiful song of a lone bird not too far in the distance. Hearing a bird sing is like hearing the Siren's call to my brain and I stopped in my tracks to tune in to the beauty of the sound. (A wonderful quote from Rumi comes to mind: "Birdsong brings relief to my longing."[6]) I listened for a while, sending my heart-felt gratitude to the singer of the song and then made my way to a table on the terrace with a clear view of the river I love so much.

I had brought some books with me by two authors who are great lights on the planet, Amelia Kinkade and Tama Kieves (see Bibliography). The energy and vibration of love that comes through their words is so astounding that, as I read, I could feel my old friends, self-doubt and insecurity, begin to awaken from their nap. I observed my mind as it asserted that I couldn't write as well as they could, and I wondered why was I even trying to write a book at all when these women could write such profound and joyous books. I indulged for a while in comparing myself to them in unflattering terms, but as the afternoon wore on, the deep peace of the garden and the love vibration of my own writing gradually dispelled the storm cloud of self-doubt. I decided to choose this peace over any fear of not being good enough, and by the time I was ready to leave I was filled with gratitude for the beauty of the song bird, for the sunlight dazzling off the river, and for life itself. This gratitude engendered the feeling that life is filled with magic! My heart was full and I could feel a great love flowing through me.

Walking the path to the garden's exit I was surprised to hear what sounded like the same bird who was singing when I came in. This time the bird was just several feet away perched on an upper branch of a small tree. It was easy to spot him and I watched for a minute as he sang his heart out. I closed my eyes and was transfixed by the call of his wildness. I was so grateful for his glorious gift, and as I attuned my mind to his, I said, "Thank you, thank you, for your song, beautiful one." He stopped singing and I heard him say, "I am here for *you* today." Stunned, I opened my eyes to look at him. He didn't sing again, and in about ten seconds he took wing. I could see him fly for a moment but then he seemed to disappear into thin air.

I was in heaven as I began the walk home on the road just beyond the garden. Not long into my walk I noticed a beautiful, small, light gray feather on the ground in front of me and I picked it up. The bird who sang for me was light gray, and I soon discovered, through a feather identification web site, that it most likely was a feather from a mockingbird. Mockingbirds can mimic and reproduce the song of many species of birds. They seem not to have their own song. Was the bird who sang for me a mockingbird, and was this one of his feathers? And if the answer to either of those questions was yes, was that significant? I'm not sure of the answer to those questions but I feel that my Spirit Bird was telling me that I didn't have to mimic the "song" of any other writer.

My heart's song, my heart's voice, is beautiful and valuable too. I can and must sing my own unique and lovely song. May you as well, dear one, sing your own unique and exquisite song, the song you were born to sing.

Another significant Spirit Animal appeared to me at the end of one of the meetings of the meditation and healing group that I facilitate at a nursing home. (I have their permission to speak about our experience.) The people who have come to the circle over several years are extraordinary souls who co-create the energy and the experiences of the group with me and with Spirit. We begin each session with relaxation exercises and several minutes of mindfulness meditation. Then we imagine combining our individual hearts into a single open heart, and we imagine bringing the earth into that heart. Enveloping the globe with the brilliant, living light of Spirit's healing love, we ask that all beings be blessed and healed including the earth herself. We envision the earth's land and plant life, her air and her waters being cleansed and purified. We ask for and envision the healing of all two-legged beings, all four-legged ones, those who fly or swim or crawl—all beings. May they all be well. May we all be well. May all hearts be healed.

During one of our meetings, as we imagined holding up the globe to receive Spirit's healing light, I was shown a stunning vision. An angelic Being of Light was holding what looked like some kind of mirror or lens over our healing intentions for the earth. This "light-being" seemed to be employing the technique of starting a fire by concentrating and focusing sunlight onto a combustible substance. I heard the words, "Spirit is intensifying your intentions to help all beings heal and awaken, and it is magnifying them in order to ignite a symbolic fire of divine love and healing in the world." I was filled with gratitude beyond words. I told the group about the vision and we shared in the joy. We were thrilled.

As we were coming to the close of our circle and beginning to come back into waking consciousness, an elephant so massive and majestic appeared in my mind. I was awestruck, and was soon informed that this breathtaking creature was our circle's Animal Spirit. I have always been in love with elephants. I'm in awe of their spirit and their power and many things I can't put into words. For all of my life, just the thought of an elephant elicits a wave of love from my heart. This love goes out not only to elephants but to all of this magical life that is made more sacred and beautiful because elephants are in it. I thanked our magnificent Animal Spirit for joining us and for supporting us.

Later that evening I researched elephant spirit guides online and was amazed to read (on the first web site that I sampled) that "by connecting to elephant spirit, **we affect planetary healing beyond the space-time continuum.**"[7] (emphasis added) Even as I write these words I get a chill of recognition from Spirit letting me know that yes, that's exactly what was happening in the group. The call of our focused love and our intentions to help the planet heal was responded to and magnified by Spirit's love. The power of this force of love is not bound by the illusions of time and space.

I offer you that what is indeed true and real is so much deeper and more miraculous and mystical than anything we've been programmed to perceive and to believe. We are limitless awareness. We are the immense power of Spirit's love in form. And our only limitation is one of *imagination*.

Spirit is whispering to you now ...

This Great Dreamer whose sweet reveries have brought Love into form from the beginning of time is dreaming of you this moment, Dear One. You cannot be lost to me because you are part of me. You are the wild call of my heart... and the response. You are my longing... and the completion. You cannot be separate from my love and neither can any creature on earth. There is no two-legged or four-legged or winged one, no being who swims or crawls or climbs, no mighty oak nor blade of grass that is apart from this love. It is the nature of reality.

*All creatures are manifesting and interpreting my love in their own unique way. Each species brings their special kind of beauty to the earth, and each sings their own song of praise and joy. All songs are Spirit's songs, and it is the spirit of this Great Lover of All that urges the precious dolphin and whale to leap and breach in utter joy over being alive. It is this spirit that urges the wild horse to gallop free across the prairie in joyful abandon. It is my spirit that glides and soars in the sky with the eagle and the falcon. And it is this same spirit, my spirit, which is within **you.** You may feel it when you're filled with joy as you look upon your newborn, or when you sing or dance from your heart, or when your heart expands with deep gratitude for the gift of life.*

The creatures of the earth are awakening like you; they are becoming conscious. Sometimes the awakening will appear to be a gradual process and sometimes it will be by leaps and bounds. The more joy you allow yourself to experience, the faster the quickening for all beings.

As has been prophesied through many indigenous peoples, you, the Rainbow Warriors, have now come to the planet because you heard the cries of the ravaged earth and her dying creatures. You have been given the power to be the voice of the voiceless, and you are imbued with the power to help all beings awaken and heal. So take heart, Beloved, because one day when compassion and understanding have replaced war and destruction and hatred, all peoples will remember themselves as One People, and even species who were extinct will return in elation to the earth.

Can you imagine it now? It is a reality that is already forming in the Mind of God, so sing, oh sing for the beauty of the earth. All is already well and you are so dearly loved.

CHAPTER VII

Uncovering the True Self

Love is
The funeral pyre
Where I have laid my living body.

All the false notions of myself
That once caused fear, pain,

Have turned to ash
As I neared God.

Hafiz[1]

Uncovering the True Self

How do we come to know and to feel that we are *love itself*? How do we go about uncovering this true Self of love that is our core? This Self is the unchangeable: the infinite consciousness and infinite love that lie beneath all of the ways we've chosen to express our individuality. So we begin this process of uncovering with an exploration of the many ways in which we've come to define ourselves and how these self-definitions have hidden the reality of who we really are.

What I refer to as our costumes and our masks make up a public persona that most of us overidentify with and mistake as our true identity. Examining the facets of this persona is the beginning of sorting out what is ephemeral and what is our true and unchangeable nature. The second stage of approach to the remembrance of the real Self is through going within ourselves in a meditative state. To fully experience the reality of our true nature, to know the stillness and peace that lie beneath our masks, we must approach the heart of mindfulness.

The Costume Party

What if the *real you* were in disguise? What if this life on the material plane were like a great big costume party that you, as a soul, chose to attend? The only way you can be admitted to this earthly party is by donning a human costume. In this case the costume is not that of some fictional or historical character. Rather the costume is your body and the details of your life situation that your higher self (your God/Goddess part) chose before you reincarnated. You chose your human costume to best suit your life experiences and spiritual needs of your lifetime.

Exploring the party analogy, imagine if you will that you're invited to attend a real costume party, and your only access into the party is to be in full disguise. No one knows who you are underneath your disguise unless you speak or in some way reveal yourself. While in costume you are treated like the character whose persona you've taken on (for example, Superman or Wonder Woman). But even in full disguise, you always know your real identity underneath it all. When you return home and remove the costume, the people around you treat you not as the costumed personality but as your original identity once again. I offer you the possibility that life on the physical plane, your physical existence, *is* like a grand and crazy costume party.

So what specific things might your costume consist of this lifetime? It would consist of all of the attributes and personal qualities that you gave your consent to before birth, such as your nationality, your gender identity and sexual orientation. It would include your appearance and all of the physical characteristics that identify you, such as dark skin or light, brown eyes or blue, tall or not so tall, and so on. Your disguise would also include your abilities, talents, any limitations or disabilities, who your parents are or were, your ancestral DNA (genetic and epigenetic heritage), even the challenges and lessons of the lifetime. It's also possible that the early childhood conditioning that molded your self-image could be part of the costume. This conditioning may have created your emotional attachments as well as your assumptions and beliefs about the nature of the world and yourself. It's all part of the disguise of your human character.

In this metaphorical costume party called Life on Planet Earth, however, we, the wearers of the disguises, forget that we're in costume. We're usually unaware that there is a deeper identity beyond the set of external characteristics and self-images of the ego. We forget our true nature as we become accustomed to the denser and lower vibration of the material plane, so that whatever roles we've taken on and the personalities we've nurtured over the years become a kind of prison. We become stuck in the roles of our disguises, which represent our egos and not our true selves. We become stuck in the illusion of a small, separate self. This is how we limit ourselves—as if we had to be Superman or Wonder Woman for our whole lives, as if we couldn't get out of character.

For instance, a limiting aspect of the costume with which most of us tend to overidentify is our being male or female (or whatever variation you identify with) and our masculinity or femininity. If we are not our costumes, though, then you and I are not *really* a man or a woman even though we appear as one this lifetime. You and I are spiritual beings of light who've taken on a body (and all of the other details of our costumes) based solely on the spiritual requirements of this lifetime's path.

We also tend to overidentify with and feel exaggerated allegiance to the nation of our birth or upbringing. Over the last several centuries, all over the world many lands and their resources have been appropriated by people who committed genocide against the indigenous peoples who'd lived there for thousands of years. Seemingly arbitrary or subjective national boundaries have then been drawn to form countries, and yet we still tend to see our own nation's citizens as separate, usually superior beings. Have you ever wondered why we feel the need to claim that our country or our city is the best in the world? Whether we define "best" to mean that our country has the highest standard of living or has the most desirable form of government, we are using the concept of competition to create a winner and a loser. Can we not just celebrate our own national uniqueness and the delightful differences among countries and cultures without needing to be "better than"?

The same can be said of religions which teach their adherents that nonbelievers are not as worthy of respect as those who have the faith or that nonbelievers will not be saved. I offer you another perhaps outrageous possibility that the only true error from which humanity needs to be saved is our not waking up to the spiritual reality of our material lives. It's reassuring to know, however, that each of us will ultimately wake up to that truth during one or another of our lifetimes.

All over the world, disturbing dramas are played out based on our unquestioned beliefs that we *are* men or women, that we *are* Americans or Russians or Chinese, that we *are* Christians or Jews or Muslims. These identifications are illusions that do not represent our essence. The wonderful external differences among us are just part of the disguises we needed to wear to come into physical life on our common, albeit temporary, home, Earth. Several years ago I was invited to a neighbor's Halloween party. (I was never comfortable with the energy surrounding the festival of Halloween and this party was the last Halloween party I ever attended.) I wore normal street clothes to the event but with one unusual accessory. I wore a sign pinned to my sweater that read, "This *is* my costume!" Only a few people understood the meaning of the message.

Please remember that you are not any of the aspects of your disguise! You are the infinite consciousness and potential which exists beneath the masks. This is the time for all of us to become aware of the costumes and masks we've worn, and how we've defined ourselves solely in their terms. At the same time, though, we aren't meant to reject our physical existence or our costumes. We're meant to remember that our costumes are only the means by which Spirit, through us, manifests its love in the physical world. We're meant to learn the lessons and experience the joy and the pleasure inherent in the opportunities that our costumes provide. The key is to consciously enjoy our physicality without overidentifying with it or with any of the disguises of the ego.

I'm reminded here of the lovely writing of Ken Carey in *Return of the Bird Tribes* who suggests that we don't have to try to suppress or transcend our ego, we just have to know that our primary identity is spiritual. In *The Starseed Transmissions,* he writes further that as we awaken to our true identity as both matter and Spirit, we begin to understand that our bodies are exquisite instruments designed for expressing God in form. "**You** are the Spirit of Life itself, dancing in the clay, delighting in the glorious opportunity of incarnation, exploring the realms of matter, blessing the earth and all therein."[2]

Taking Off the Masks of Our Costumes

As I have mentioned earlier, once upon a time the universe helped me to co-create a life situation of chronic, debilitating illness that forced me to confront the myriad "masks" I had grown accustomed to wearing. A mask, by definition, is something we wear that hides what is true underneath, and with the exception of living saints, we all wear masks as part of our costume. Essentially our masks are the life roles we play and their corresponding self-images. They're developed throughout our upbringing as the mind creates a conception of who we and our families think we are and who we think we need to be in the world.

With the advent of chronic, undiagnosed disease and severe clinical depression, I could no longer maintain the idea of myself as good worker, good student, good friend or attractive woman. Those roles and the sense of self-worth they afforded me were simply dissolved. With the demise of my masks I was forced to experience my life without the familiar ways in which I had defined myself. As it turned out, having those limited but comfortable self-definitions pulled out from under me turned out to be a true blessing in disguise. The experience of being rejected by friends, a lover, and people at school helped me to realize that I was more than the parts I played on my life's stage. I discovered that I was much more than any way I had chosen to characterize myself.

There are different layers of masks we wear, and the most basic kind is the mask of being "only human." As we grow up and acquire the trappings of our culture, most of us forget that we are here on earth as spiritual beings in costume, so to speak. We forget that we are infinite awareness beneath the guise of our humanness.

We wear many personality masks as well. These masks represent our attachment to the self-images and identifications we believe we need just to feel good enough or normal enough to fit in. Our masks allow us to project a certain image to others and to ourselves that serves to protect our often fragile sense of self. In my case, as with so many of us, that sense of self was fragile because I'd been brought up without the knowledge of my own inherent goodness. On some level I grew up believing that I was somehow to blame for others' unhappiness and that I was fundamentally bad. Feeling desperate to belong and be accepted by my family and their world, I constantly tried to be something that I believed I was not—everything that was good and without blame. Looking back on my life I can see that the masks I wore (and some I still wear) were a direct result of not knowing that I and everyone else had been born with Original Blessing (a concept popularized by Matthew Fox) instead of the mythical Original Sin. Growing up I didn't know about the innocence and purity of my own heart and neither did my parents know of theirs.

There is nothing inherently good or bad about our masks, however. They're just the ways we've been taught to see ourselves. They're just the limiting labels we've been taught to apply to who and how we think we need to be. The problem is that we're not conscious of the mind's construction of the "self" and its resulting masks. We begin to believe that we must be—and *must be seen as*—whatever quality or trait our family or our society values. We suffer if the self-images that our masks represent are challenged by others or are just too difficult to keep up. For example, we may need to wear the mask of the always-good mother or father or the always-good friend or spouse in order to feel okay about ourselves. Or we may feel the need to perceive ourselves and to be perceived by others as being always honest or competent or loving. If we are attached to the belief that we are (and have to be) always honest or loving, then who are we when we're inevitably not?

We might feel insulted if someone challenges our integrity. Feeling insulted or experiencing any kind of emotional pain from our attachment to our self-definitions is a form of suffering, and so much suffering comes from trying to hold the construct of "me" intact and defended. So much energy goes into the perceived need to protect our cherished self-images from external confrontations and inner confusion.

Sometimes our masks or personas are aspects of our defense mechanisms, unconscious ways our early childhood mind learned to defend and protect itself from overwhelming pain and anxiety. As I mentioned in Chapter 1, transpersonal psychologist, John Welwood, has described how, as children, we learn to shut down and contract around painful feelings out of fear of feeling overwhelmed by them. Unless we learn to pay loving attention to that fear and pain as adults, we continue to avoid those experiences that caused us distress. We continue to constrict ourselves as we try to shore up an *incomplete* identity since we've identified only with those aspects of our experience that we're comfortable with and have defended against those that we're not. As an example, if a child is shamed for crying, he or she may soon feel anxiety when showing or even feeling sadness or vulnerability. If that anxiety is uncomfortable enough, the mind will unconsciously deny even the experience of sadness and vulnerability. A mask, a facade, of invulnerability has just been put on. According to Dr. Welwood,

"In this way we become disabled, unable to function in areas of our lives that evoke feelings we've never learned to tolerate. Turning away from this primary pain creates a second, ongoing level of suffering: living in a state of contraction and constricted awareness."[3]

Our masks are rooted in our fear—fear of not belonging and of not being loved, and that fear can be powerful. It can motivate us to shore up those "faces" that we originally felt we needed to show to our caregivers and the world around us and now feel the need to show to ourselves. That fear and the masks it produces persist until, through self-compassion or *maitri*, "placing our fearful mind in the cradle of loving kindness,"[4] as Pema Chödrön describes, we can bring the masks into our conscious awareness. Ultimately our masks keep us separate from our own feelings, from others, and from the reality of our own basic goodness.

As we become more conscious we begin to realize that there is no single way we need to be or need to be seen as, except exactly who we are in any given moment. As we become more awake to our own innate purity, our own Buddha-nature, we understand that we are not our thoughts, we are not our emotions, and we are not our behavior. Those things are temporary phenomena, arising and passing away. We are instead the awareness and the love underneath all that we experience. In the awakened state we can redirect the tremendous energy that goes into keeping our masks in place and use it for the journey toward mindfulness and authenticity. We will then have freed ourselves up to become who we came here to be, and who we came here to be is so much more magnificent than any mask could represent.

This is the challenge of each lifetime: to cut through the illusions of our facades, the masks we show the world and ourselves. We are now in the very midst of that awakening to our deeper identity, our *true* identity beneath the images we project of who we imagine we need to be. When we can have compassion for ourselves, we can recognize the false identities we've clung to, and we can begin the process of relinquishing them. We can begin to come back to the memory of the original blamelessness and blessedness, innocence and limitless potential that we came into this world with. We can then enjoy the true freedom and joy that living an authentic and open-hearted life allows.

Over the years there've been writers whose words and energy have helped me to better understand the relationship between the roles of our ego and our infinite Self. Ken Carey is one of those writers. In *The Starseed Transmissions,* he suggests that in a state of awakened grace, our masks or false identifications fall away and a new identity comes into place:

> "This identity will not be an exclusive identity that feels separation from the rest of its kind, but a cooperative identity that **understands its own uniqueness to be the mechanism through which it might serve the greater whole.**"[5] [emphasis added]

The Chalice: Taking Off Another Mask

The very first college class I taught with my brand new Ph.D. was an evening class on The Psychology of Aging at a New York college. The very first student to enter the room that evening was a serious and dignified, well-dressed, middle-aged lady named Ruth. She sat front and center and observed me closely. Years later she would tell me that her heart sank with dismay during that first class when she saw me "flip my long blond hair back" in what she believed to be a gesture of vain superficiality. She assumed that I would be an airhead! Not long into the semester, though, she decided that that was not the case.

Ruth was part of a handful of students who stayed after class at ten p.m. every week to meditate with me. I was so impressed with that group and I so respected them. Many of them worked full-time jobs while pursuing their education in the evening. Yet they were willing to spend an extra hour at night, after a long day, to meditate. Over the semester we explored different meditative techniques and discussed spiritual theory. I offered everything only as food for thought, not as anyone else's reality other than my own.

Ruth and I stayed in touch after the end of that semester, as we shared a special love of elders. As time went by we grew close, and we often laughed about her apprehension over my toss-of-the-hair gesture which I didn't remember but would try to recreate for her amusement. We continued to meditate together for more than twenty years, initially as part of a group that I facilitated and then in later years, as just the two of us. We'd come together once a week or so to meditate and pray for people we knew personally and for people in the world and ultimately for all beings. For us, praying involved our sending out the energy and vision of what we felt was living light and healing love to others. We also visualized whomever we were praying for as already healed and already whole, which is how we all exist in the Universal Mind.

We would begin our meditation by withdrawing our attention from the stimuli of the external world and refocusing that attention within ourselves. We made the conscious decision to allow the outer world to go on without us for a little while as we eased ourselves into that infinite and compassionate spaciousness within our own hearts. As we relaxed, our attention would come to focus on our breath, and using a classic mindfulness meditation technique, we would note the sensations of the breath as it came in and went out through the nostrils. As thoughts or feelings or sensations from the body arose we released awareness of them and gently guided the attention back to the breath.

Eventually we would access a deeply quiet state of mind and heart where we could feel a connection to some form of higher consciousness and its inherent wisdom. And *always* there would be this tremendous feeling of intense, compassionate love flowing through us for any and all of those for whom we prayed. It didn't matter who the recipients of our prayer were; we could feel that all beings were dearly loved and we could feel it deep down to our bones. We could hear Spirit calling all of us "Beloveds." We soon got into the habit of referring to each person and each being as our beloved. We might say, for example, "We put our beloved Catherine or our beloved Michael (or whomever we were praying for) in the living light of Spirit's love."

It has always amazed me how powerful language is in shaping our thoughts and our beliefs, which then ultimately become the very fabric of our lives. As we continued to think of even so-called strangers or the world's (or history's) purported villains as our cherished ones, it became more and more difficult to consider anyone as being an outsider—as being outside of our personal circle of loved ones. If *all beings* are Spirit's beloveds, how could we exclude anyone from the realm of our love and compassion? At least that's how we felt while we were in the altered state. It wasn't always easy to hold on to that feeling when we were back in our quotidian existence, but we did the best that we could in that regard.

Frequently we received messages from the spiritual realm relating to the people for whom we were praying and sometimes relating to ourselves. The information was often very specific, and we always relayed any message to its recipient with a caveat: *please take only what resonates in you of what may come through us, and leave the rest.*

Once while we were meditating together several years ago, Ruth was told that on a specific date in the near future I'd be receiving a significant message from Spirit. We tried to elicit further information, even a hint or two about the subject of the communication, but nothing more was forthcoming. When that day arrived I remembered Ruth's words, and while riding the train to my Manhattan office I turned within myself to try to ascertain Spirit's message. I asked to receive some kind of communication from the higher realms, and as I opened myself to the response, a scene began to unfold in my mind.

The scene involved me sitting across from a radiant Being of Light who was drinking wine from a shiny gold chalice. He drank the chalice dry and handed it to me. I understood that there was no more liquid in the bowl of the chalice, and as I accepted it from him, I felt I should peer into it. My expectation was to look into the shiny golden interior of the chalice and see the reflection of my face. But when I looked inside, the interior metal was neither shiny nor gold. There was a dull, matte surface within the chalice—like pewter— and I could not see my own reflection! In the fraction of a second I felt a wave of electric fear flow through my body. My instinctive reaction was the feeling that if there were no reflection to be seen, then *I must not be. I must not exist.* For a few moments the fear of annihilation and nonbeing gripped my stomach.

But as I sat with the fear, allowing myself to experience it, it began to dissipate, and I remembered that the individual ego is useful for living on the material plane but it's impermanent. The idea that one is *only* a unique individual, completely separate from all others and from all of life, is an illusion. Therefore, the fact that I could not see my reflection became not so much fearsome, but rather informative. Informing and reminding me on a deep level that my life is not only about me with my distinct individuality, my being "Sheila," but about my—and our—*connectedness* to something larger than ourselves, something more inclusive, something universal.

I also remembered that soon after I began to wake up and become more conscious many years ago, some part of my deeper self understood that I had already committed this lifetime to the purposes of Spirit long before I'd reincarnated. Now living this life, I felt compelled to reaffirm the offer of this lifetime back to Spirit. Not seeing my face in the cup of the chalice was simply a confirmation of this. I still have a choice, but it feels like since I had made the commitment to the divine, there was no turning back. I had "signed the sacred contract" on the other side for the spiritually meaningful life where my uniqueness and my ego is expressed in service to Spirit, and since coming back to the earth, I've recommitted to it. Again I'm reminded of the gorgeous words of Ken Carey (in *The Third Millennium*):

> "Within you the Starmaker trembles on the threshold of awakening. Your ego will not dissolve in such an awakening; it will ascend into enlightened comprehension of its cocreative partnership with the Eternal Being in whom this universe congeals."[6]

I had a dream not long after the experience with the chalice that underscored its message. In the dream I was at a costume party. I was dressed in street clothes but had a large empty pitcher hanging around my neck. A Medicine Woman came up to me and told me that this pitcher, this empty vessel, was my costume this lifetime. For many years now, one of my daily affirmations has been that I am an empty vessel through which Spirit works and through which Spirit heals.

The recommitment is active and on-going. I continue to say to Spirit, "Whatever you want me to do, I'll do it, as long as it feels right to me. Wherever I can be of greatest service, send me there. I can be dense and headstrong so you will have to guide me and make it crystal clear what is wanted of me. I will listen as best I can to the still, small voice in my heart for your guidance, and then I will do what feels right to me in that regard. If I should go off course I trust that you will redirect me back to the path."

Before I get out of bed in the morning, I do my best to remember to affirm two things: "I commit this day to the service of fulfilling my spiritual contract (whatever it may be)" and "I accept complete karmic responsibility for everything that I co-create with Spirit today." In my understanding, karmic responsibility means that absolutely nothing that happens is random, and that we co-create our world and our life events with Spirit and with others, even if we don't know how we're doing it. Most saliently here, everything that you and I co-create is somehow for our higher, spiritual good, and very often what's created is giving us a golden opportunity to learn compassion. Please let your imagination at least allow for the possibility of this spiritual truth: that things don't happen to you, they happen *for* you, and your own soul has drawn them to you. Speaking of things happening for our higher good, Tama Kieves suggests that when we are true to ourselves, when we support ourselves and honor our instincts, "it's a path of unwavering good, though we may have to deepen into our awareness of that good."[7] I smile with her statement since that deepening can take a lot of practice!

Spirit whispers to you now...

Dear One, can you allow yourself to reconnect with the exquisite beauty of who you really are beneath the veneer of your costume? You are my Beloved, and you and all beings are being supported by this universe in all ways as you struggle to become awake and aware of your true and sacred Self.

Long before this lifetime you and the others here agreed to be on the earth at this time. You decided, with great determination and great generosity of heart, to support each other and yourself in awakening from the long slumber of forgetfulness and unconsciousness. You are sleeping giants beginning to rouse and remove your masks, and you have come together to create nothing less than planetary and cosmic history.

May all beings remember ever more fully, ever more deeply, their true nature. May all beings know their infinite consciousness and infinite goodness beneath their masks. And may all who have life share in the grace of our coming together through these words today.

CHAPTER VIII

Whispers of Love from the Deeper Self

You are the means by which God loves Creation…
You are high priests and priestesses, invested
with the authority to perform
the only real Mass,
the Cosmic Mass of the World,
in which Matter is lifted up lovingly into
the Presence of God, and instilled with
the power and the life of Spirit.

Ken Carey[1]

A Tale of Resistance: The Raisin and Me

Who would have thought that an encounter with a shriveled little piece of fruit would become an impetus for further awakening and healing for me? But it was, and I bless it for that. The lesson of a raisin remains somewhere in the back of my mind, reminding me to pay loving attention to Whatever Is in the present moment.

Several years ago I had the pleasure of attending a week-long retreat which focused on the practice of mindfulness, the practice of being *here now*, of being present within our experience on a moment to moment basis. The setting of the retreat, a beautiful and serene conference center, made it a little easier to attempt this than in the midst of our normally busy lives. To further reduce distractions, no radio or TV or computer was allowed, and we were asked to avoid using our phones if possible.

There were over 100 participants at the retreat and some had never meditated before. I had been meditating for about fifteen years at that point, doing a little mindfulness meditation but mostly using a mantra to focus and calm my mind. I'd had those mystical, transcendent experiences during the early years of meditating that had changed my life, and I considered myself fairly spiritually advanced (I'm less advanced now!). I was hoping the retreat would be an opportunity to hone my meditation skills. I was anticipating neither revelation nor healing.

After early morning yoga, we practiced "sitting mindfulness meditation" throughout the day and evening, where we were to bring our attention to the sensations of the breath coming in and going out. As we meditated, other perceptions would arise in consciousness, such as sensations or thoughts or feelings. When we became aware that our attention had shifted to something other than the sensations of the breath, we were to gently guide the awareness back to its original focus. This sitting meditation was occasionally interspersed with walking meditation—where we practiced bringing the same observant awareness to the moment to moment experience of putting one foot in front of the other.

Part of being mindful, of being present, means that we allow ourselves to acknowledge—with compassion—our very real resistance to the awareness and flow of our own feelings. It involves having the courage to go into our soft, tender heart to face our fears of feeling what we feel. Getting to that inner spaciousness may involve sitting in mindful silence for prolonged periods of time, allowing the scattered mind to begin to quiet down. When that quieting does happen, the vestiges of accumulated painful reactions and perceptions—our resistances—may start to bubble up into conscious awareness. These perceptions and insights may be emotions or memories, things we've tried to keep at arm's length out of fear of feeling the hurt again. During this retreat we were occasionally privy to the surfacing of *otherwise private* painful or poignant insights of some of the other participants; we could hear their sobbing.

During a noon break in the middle of the week, the facilitator asked if anyone would like to share their experience of the morning's meditation. An attractive middle aged man volunteered that he'd been crying that morning because he'd had a profound realization. He told us that he was not a meditator, and that he'd just wanted to accompany his beautiful wife to the retreat. He was a successful and respected professional with wonderful children. He had a great life—and he'd just realized that he'd not been *truly present* for a single moment of it!

One afternoon we were given an exercise in mindfulness that involved each of us receiving two raisins. We were instructed to take one of the raisins and just "be with" it. To begin that process, we were to look at the raisin as if we'd never seen one before. We were to notice all its little ridges and valleys and to really *see* this object and its essence as if for the first time. Then we were to allow ourselves to really feel what a raisin felt like in our hand, as if we'd never felt one before. We were to notice if its flesh was yielding or firm, what the tips of our fingers felt like holding this little object, what temperature it was, and so on.

We were then asked to go through the process of ingesting the raisin as mindfully as possible, in extremely slow motion. First we raised the raisin to our lips and let our lips truly feel what it felt like. Then we placed the raisin on our tongue, just noticing the sensation of it resting there. The next step involved putting the raisin between our teeth, but not chewing it. We then slowly applied pressure to the raisin and finally began to chew. We chewed exceedingly slowly until we had finally swallowed the last bit of raisin with careful awareness. I'm not sure exactly how long the exercise lasted, but it felt like several minutes.

The final stage of the exercise began with our being asked to take the second raisin we'd been given and go through the same mindful process with it. I instantly rejected the idea of doing the exercise again. The very first thought I had was that I didn't want to ingest the extra calories of another raisin (really, no kidding), and I decided that I just didn't have the patience to go through the whole procedure one more time. So I quickly slipped the second raisin into my pocket! After the rest of the group had finished their sequence with the second raisin, the facilitator asked us to consider what, if anything, we had resisted about the exercise.

I was stunned. What did I resist??? "You resisted the WHOLE THING!" I scolded myself. I just couldn't understand why I had refused a perfectly benign experience and the flow of its feeling through my consciousness. There seemed to be no good reason for my refusal, other than some vague sense of discomfort and anxiety.

My reaction to that exercise shook me up, and I began to wonder just how many other things I was resisting because of some hidden, unconscious motivation. Many examples, some small and some significant, began to cascade through my mind of experiences that I had defended against throughout my life. With some alarm I recalled events and people, emotions and thoughts that I had avoided (or tried to avoid) for a lifetime out of some half-realized, diffuse fear of pain that I couldn't articulate.

With hindsight, however, I've come to realize there were some powerful feelings just under the surface of my conscious mind, feelings that I was afraid I couldn't handle if they were allowed into perception. I'm sure that one layer of feeling had to do with a life-long, painful issue with food, as evidenced by my concern over the caloric content of a raisin. Apparently, that concern was a rationalization that had helped me to hide my feelings from myself.

Memories began to surface of having gorged myself on raisins and other foods as a young teenager. I'm certain that compulsive overeating was an attempt to numb my emotional pain. The numbing effect, though, was always very brief, and the shame of having lost control with food only made me feel worse about myself. Of course the struggle with food (or any other substance or activity) is just a symptom of some deeper pain. It's a signal from the deeper self that lets us know that something— emotional and spiritual—has fallen out of balance. The signal is asking us to pay *loving* attention—nonjudgmental attention—to whatever we feel. It is this compassionate attention that helps us begin to restore the balance.

I understand now that the deeper feelings I was afraid to acknowledge were usually ones of grief and rage, unworthiness and shame that had originated and taken root in my early childhood. Evidently, the remnants of those old feelings were still alive and well within me, and my resisting a raisin had begun the process of bringing them out of the dark corners of my psyche and into the light of awareness to be healed.

The exercise with the raisin was a truly humbling experience, reminding me that I was not as evolved as I'd thought. It also reminded me that wherever we go we take our resistances and our shadow side with us—those layers of repressed feelings and self-identifications that are contrary to the self-image we prefer to hold about ourselves. The layers represent parts of ourselves which we have unconsciously denied and disowned because they frighten and repel us. But *because we are meant to heal* on all levels, evidence of these layers will inevitably surface into waking consciousness, often when we least expect it or want it. When an aspect of our shadow side does break through into consciousness, all we can do is acknowledge its message with gratitude and compassion so that it can be understood and integrated into our whole selves. All we can do is open our hearts to ourselves and our woundedness once again, and accept our woundedness as part of a shared, human condition.

In the years since then, the training in mindfulness has been an invaluable tool for me in the process of learning to become conscious of what I'm really feeling and thinking and perceiving. It's a process of allowing myself to become conscious of what's really going on just beneath the surface of my fearful defendedness. Actually, the practice of being here now and doing my best to have utter compassion for whatever I find within myself in the present moment has become the cornerstone of my spiritual practice. I do wish I could say that having that compassion for myself under all circumstances is easy, though. It isn't. Sometimes I just can't manage it. I'm a work in progress like you. But at least I try to muster some gentleness for the part of me that doesn't always feel worthy of compassion.

A few years after the retreat I was part of a group who volunteered at the maximum security correctional facility, Sing Sing, in Westchester County, New York. Once, as part of a presentation I gave on mindfulness, I told my raisin resistance story to a group of inmates and volunteers. One of the volunteers had the courage to tell me (in front of everyone else) "Don't feel bad. I have a *pocketful* of raisins!"

Whispers from the Deeper Self

All pain or discomfort is a sign from the deeper self that lets us know that something has fallen out of balance. For example, if we were having a heart attack, we might feel pressure in our chest or pain that radiates to our jaw or down our left arm. These symptoms would be a signal to us that something was wrong with the heart. Or if our appendix were about to burst we might feel a persistent, intense pain in the lower right abdomen and have a high fever. Again, pain and fever would be functioning as indicators to get our attention and to let us know that something wasn't right. Emotional pain as well is a sign from a deeper part of ourselves that lets us know that an imbalance exists and asks us to pay loving attention to it. This nonjudgmental attention to all that we feel starts the process of restoring the equilibrium.

Ultimately, all imbalance and disharmony have their origin on the spiritual level, and reflect our loss of conscious awareness of and trust in our spiritual Source. As the disharmony progresses, our deeper self gives us hints and whispers (even before the experience of pain) to let us know that the harmony is lost and to ask us to bring our awareness to the situation. These hints and whispers may be perceived as a feeling of uneasiness or distress or as a vague intuition that something is amiss.

We don't always want to pay conscious attention to the whispers, however, and we may move quickly into denial about their authenticity. We may be afraid to acknowledge and feel the discomfort or the hurt of certain emotions, perhaps because we don't want to admit that we're capable of all the same thoughts and feelings and impulses as everyone else. We may fear that we'll be overwhelmed by grief or that we don't have the necessary skills to deal effectively with whatever hurts. Or we may not have the courage to do what we know we must to change a painful situation. Since the purpose of the pain is only to invite us to pay attention to the underlying disharmony for the purpose of healing, its whisper—if avoided or denied—usually becomes louder and more insistent.

Since thoughts and feelings are a form of energy, the energy of *habitual* ways of thinking and feeling will eventually manifest on the material plane in one way or another. So we may experience the more insistent whispers from the deeper self in the form of such things as our recurring dramas, our addictions, or our illnesses. But beneath all of the whispers is the soul's longing to restore the original balance and harmony—the remembrance of our spiritual nature and our true power, which is to create the vibration of love. The balance can be restored only through *facing* and releasing our fears, and through identifying with the pure, open, and nonjudgmental awareness that underlies all experience. As we do this, we come to understand that all emotions and thoughts are just energies that flow through us and that we don't need to contract around them or defend against them. Ultimately we will uncover the awareness of Spirit's living presence and love within us. This process, with its innate vibration of love, *begins with whatever fearless compassion we can muster for ourselves.*

Spirit is whispering to you ....

Beloved, the Joyous One who whispered creation into being is whispering to you now: Take my hand as we drift and spiral up into the stars. Take my hand as we glide through space on cosmic thermals like eagles gliding over the universe. Let your being hear my whisper—that you are safe, that you are loved, that you are love itself. All is already well, Beloved.

Opening Our Hearts to Ourselves

Generating the vibration of love is the foundation of our true power and our true healing, and it begins with awareness and the *opening of our hearts to ourselves.* Anything we resist—any feeling or experience that we try to keep out of consciousness—keeps us out of our own heart. We may even believe that, in effect, there are two doors to the heart—one marked Joy and Happiness and one marked Sorrow and Grief. We may believe that if we keep the door to sorrow closed we will experience only joy. In reality, though, there is only one door to the heart. If we close the door to the full experience of our pain, we've closed the door to all of our feelings, including the full experience of the joy and even rapture that life wants to give us. And how powerful we are when we can say, I feel this, and what I feel is my truth in this moment. Our truth in any given moment is our authenticity, our "showing up real" in our own lives.

When we pay loving attention to ourselves, we give ourselves permission to be with and stay with whatever feelings are being experienced. Loving attention means that we don't need to make a judgment about the rightness or wrongness of our feelings, nor do we need to reach for something (like food or alcohol or other drugs) that will make us numb to them. It means that we try to come to ourselves just as we are with utter compassion—not an easy task in our conditioned world. As we have the courage to pay gentle, *merciful* attention to whatever we feel, we discover that maybe we don't have to be afraid—that we're still all right no matter what emotion is surfacing. We discover that since our feelings and thoughts can change from moment to moment, they are not our essence; they are just a form of energy moving through us.

137

When we find the courage to allow ourselves to truly feel and honor what we find within, we begin to soften to our vulnerable selves. We begin to feel the attraction of merciful understanding for ourselves. And since compassion *is* the vibration of love, we have thus begun to remember what it feels like to be loved. We've begun to remember the unending love that Spirit feels for us, right this moment and always.

Ultimately we will reconnect with the love that we are, and as we do that, we will heal our sense of being cut off and separate from the rest of life and from our true Self. This healing of our sense of separateness is what the soul yearns for. Through paying compassionate attention to all that we find within ourselves, we begin to remember that we're powerful beings of Spirit's light and love who have chosen to come to the earth to bear witness to this love.

Back to the Heart
I have lived on the lip of insanity, wanting to know reasons, knocking on a door. It opens. I have been knocking from the inside!
Rumi[2]

One afternoon during those months and years when I was so ill for so long, when the days all seemed to run together in a hazy veil of unreality and pain, I began to notice that my intention to further explore this phenomenon called meditation was surfacing into conscious awareness in a fairly insistent way. Searching for some sort of instructional book, anything with a little insight or guidance on just how to begin to meditate, I made my way through dusty volumes in old bookcases until I found what I was looking for—a little paperback on the fundamentals of meditation. I had bought the book years before but had never read it, and as I thumbed through its pages, the title of one chapter caught my attention. It read, Opening the Third Eye. I wasn't exactly sure what this third eye was, but the words had piqued my interest on an intuitive level—that *feeling* that there's something energetic, something significant arising in the moment, even if you can't give words to what you feel. And yes, there *was* something energetic about to arise—literally—in my body/mind. I was about to have another mystical experience, something that would alter my understanding of life and reality once again.

Holding this little book in my hands I knew that I would have to read quickly since the ability to focus my eyes was something I could not count on with any reliability. Lying on my back (some days it took too much energy to sit up), I read a little bit about this invisible, spiritual third eye that represents one of the chakras, the centers of consciousness and subtle energy along the body and beyond. There are seven major chakras associated with the body, and the third eye is the sixth. It's associated with the point on the forehead that's just above the point between the eyebrows, and it's related to clairvoyance and intuition, among other things.

I read a line or two of the instructions on how to open the chakra, then put the book down and began the exercise that was supposed to coax open this energetic eye. I don't remember the instructions verbatim but I believe there was something about closing your eyes, deeply relaxing, and drawing awareness up from your body to focus it on the "screen of your mind." I began to feel as if energy and light were somehow opening up my head, and soon it felt like my forehead had disappeared. I realize now that with these sensations, I had been half-consciously making the assumption that this figurative eye would open out onto the world, perhaps enabling me to see more clearly, more deeply into some external reality. I was mistaken.

There really aren't adequate words to explain what happened next, but words will have to do to describe the ineffable and the indescribable. On the third attempt to follow the directions of this eye-opening lesson, my attention was suddenly drawn to a tingling, a kind of energy buzz all the way down at the end of my spine. No sooner had I become aware that something extraordinary was taking place at the base of my spine—that some kind of "geometric" energy or consciousness was coming together within me—than this tingling energy began to take shape, as if it were alive. It was forming itself into a luminous, whirling ball of light which then quickly tumbled and whirled its way up my spine and through my head until it burst itself into my inner vision. At first all that I could see in my mind's eye was brilliant, blinding light. The light was so bright I actually squinted as if that would've had some effect on this inner light.

The next phase of this experience is apparently a product of one's upbringing. Within a few seconds, stepping out of this dazzling light was the image of a radiant and gentle Christ, looking lovingly at me. I was stunned by the vision. But before I continue with the thread of the story I need to say that, since I had no context within which to understand this experience, I did some reading afterward to try to make sense of it. I read that when you have an experience of this kind, you will frequently have a vision of the avatar that represents the religion of your family of origin. If you were Buddhist, for example, you would see an image of the Buddha, or if you were Hindu, you might have a vision of Krishna. Since I'd been raised as a Christian, it was an image of Christ that appeared out of the brilliance.

I was spellbound seeing Christ, but as the vision dissolved into the background, I soon became aware that another event was energetically coming forward. My attention was drawn to and then riveted on the outline of a shimmering and vibrating circle of light coming forward. As soon as the full circle took shape, points of light seemed to pop out of the circle. These points of light shimmered and sparkled like starlight for a moment and then receded. The first one shone its light in the upper left hand quadrant of this mental

140

canvas. Then another point of bright light burst through the lower right hand quadrant. In quick succession four more points of light shone out of this curtain of light until all the points, while twinkling and receding, formed a shimmering and dazzling six-pointed star of light.

The six-pointed star with its intersecting triangles is one of the spiritual symbols of the heart chakra. The heart chakra, sometimes referred to as the heartmind, is the center of the first seven major chakras, representing the union and balance of spirit and matter (with three chakras above and three below) as well as the union of the sacred feminine (yin) and the sacred masculine (yang) energies (the left side of the body and the right). We speak of opening our heart to someone or we may say My heart goes out to him or her. Here in the heart center we find the desire and the ability to love without fear. Here we feel the energetic interconnectedness of all of life. Within the open heart we find inclusiveness instead of rejection, cooperation instead of competition, and kindness and compassion for the suffering of all of life.

Later I learned that my experience was one of Kundalini energy rising. Kundalini is a primal, vital force of energy that remains dormant and coiled at the base of the spine until it is awakened. Further, what I came to understand from this dramatic rising of energy and the vision of the six-pointed star of light was that I'd been living a life where my heart was closed—closed first and foremost to myself. When a child is conditioned, as I was, to believe that she does not possess a *basic goodness* as the foundation of her existence, she's going to close down and armor her heart. She does this to help her avoid feeling the grief and shame that a belief like that engenders, and she does it in an attempt to prevent further hurt.

For so many years I believed that I couldn't risk living with an unprotected tender heart; I couldn't risk the pain of being so vulnerable. The thing is, though, we *are* vulnerable and tender-hearted beings, even when we're trying to deny or reject the premise. We are capable of being hurt, and when we feel safe enough and strong enough to acknowledge that, we've started to heal.

Since we're not meant to live armored and closed in on ourselves, the universe often helps us to co-create some kind of healing crisis to shake us up and wake us up to how we've been living. This conscious universe knew that I needed to start healing on all levels beginning with my heart, and it helped me to co-create the physical and emotional emergency (chronic, undiagnosed illness) that would finally get my attention. Through using the exercise of opening the third eye, I was shown the "in-sight" that the truth is within us and it is heart-based; it cannot be discovered or remembered through intellectual analysis only. The truth that I needed to see and feel was that I had shut down to my feelings and thus to my aliveness. Spirit showed me that the way back to life was through opening and honoring my heart.

The Vibration of Love

Imagine yourself, Dear One, a luminous, radiant Being of Light whose true power lies in the capacity to generate the vibration of love.

How can we manifest the vibration of love in our everyday lives?

When you can summon the bravery to open your heart to *all* that you feel and pay loving attention to it—then you are manifesting the vibration of love.

When you can see your pain not just as personal to you, but as part of the whole human condition—actually as part of all of life—then you are manifesting the vibration of love.

When you can acknowledge and release whatever you're afraid of—whatever that may be—then you are manifesting the vibration of love.

When you can forgive yourself for something you've said or done (or neglected to say or do) that you deeply regret—then you are manifesting the vibration of love.

When you can find the courage to say, "Yes, that in him or her is like *this* in me"—then you are manifesting the vibration of love.

When you can try to understand and empathize with another's pain, when you try to imagine yourself in another's life circumstances—then you are manifesting the vibration of love.

When you can celebrate another's joy or prosperity, especially if it's difficult to do so—then you are manifesting the vibration of love.

When you can make the decision to be nonjudgmental about

another's life, no matter the outward appearance of things—then you are manifesting the vibration of love.

When you can summon the strength to refrain from taking advantage of another's vulnerability—then you are manifesting the vibration of love.

When you can have the presence of mind and find the strength to counter a verbal attack with compassion and kindness instead of reciprocal insults—then you are manifesting the vibration of love.

When you can come to the realization and remembrance that *all* humans deserve respect and not judgment, and that all nonhuman creatures deserve guardianship and not domination—then you are manifesting the vibration of love.

Wouldn't it change *everything* if you and I filled the world with the vibration of love?

Wouldn't it change *everything*...

> if our culture routinely rewarded us for what really matters: mercy, generosity, and humility, instead of often reinforcing actions based on greed, cruelty, and the misuse of power?

Wouldn't it change *everything* ...

> if our culture consistently rewarded us for collaboration instead of competition?

Wouldn't it change *everything* ...

> if we were encouraged in our daily lives to perform selfless acts of kindness instead of being encouraged to only look out for "Number One?"

Wouldn't it change *everything* in your life if you really *knew*...

> that you are a sacred and immortal being of light—*no matter who you are in the eyes of society?*

Wouldn't it change *everything* if you really *knew*...

> that the living and conscious planet Earth cherishes your presence as a unique expression of divine love—*no matter where you are on your journey?*

Wouldn't it change *everything* if you really *knew*...

> that the only authentic power in your life is to remember Spirit's limitless love and then to bring this love into form through what you create?

Wouldn't it change *everything* in your life if you could *feel*—deep down in your bones ...

> that you are loved by Spirit without reservation or hesitation—just as you are?

Wouldn't it change *everything* if you could *feel*—deep down in your bones ...

> that at this very moment, you are being embraced by Beings of Light whose sole purpose is to love you and support you?

Wouldn't it change *everything* if you could *feel*—deep down in your bones ...

> that you carry within you Spirit's original *blessing* and not a mythical original sin?

Wouldn't that change **everything**?

Won't it change everything when all of us remember...

> that after the body dies and we've made our transition to the other side, we will have the opportunity to review all of the events of this lifetime. This life review will allow us to see and re-experience each time we gave gentleness and understanding or indifference and cruelty to another being. We will then get to *feel* that love or pain given to others *as they experienced it.*

Won't it change everything when we remember...

> that there is nothing to fear; that this life review is done in an atmosphere of deep compassion for us. There are no judgments made; there is only our awareness of pervasive unconditional love.

Won't it change everything when we remember...

> that, ultimately, it is we who evaluate our own lives, not some vengeful deity, and that the primary and most significant "accomplishment" on which we will assess our lifetime is the amount of loving kindness we were able to give to the beings in our world and to ourselves. Selfless kindness and the profound realization that all of us sentient beings are intimately and irrevocably connected and are worthy of love is all that will truly matter at the end of our lives.

Welcoming Yourself Home ... Back into Your Own Sacred Heart

Spirit is whispering to you now ...

Welcome home, Dear One. Right here and right now, there are Beings of Light embracing you with unfathomable love, cheering you on as you awaken to the memory of your true identity and your true purity of heart. Right here in this perfect present moment, Spirit is surrounding you and lifting you up with the sweetest of heaven's sounds, and carrying you over the hard parts as you make your way back to where you started—to the loving and infinite heart of Spirit.

You are my heart, Beloved. Whoever you are in the eyes of the world, ***you are my heart and I am yours.*** *And you are a being of immense power. The power of the light of Love to create heaven on earth* ***shines through you*** *this very moment. The power of the music of Love to help heal the woundedness of all hearts (including your own)* ***flows through you*** *this very moment. You are a radiant spiritual being who couldn't wait to come to the earth to share the love that you are, and now is the time to remember. Now is the time to reconnect with the truth that reverberates within every cell and consciousness of your body:*

the truth that all beings are precious to Spirit, and that all beings are dearly loved.

the truth that ***you*** *are precious to Spirit, and that* ***you*** *are dearly loved.*

You are so dearly loved.

ENDNOTES

Acknowledgments

1. Hafiz, *The Gift: Poems by Hafiz the Great Sufi Master*, trans. Daniel Ladinsky (New York: Penguin Compass, 1999), 121.

Introduction

1. Shunryu Suzuki, *Zen Mind, Beginner's Mind* (New York: Weatherhill, 1994), 21.
2. Martin Luther King, Jr., "Why Jesus Called a Man a Fool." August 27, 1967, Sermon delivered at Mt. Pisgah Missionary Baptist Church, Chicago Illinois. https://kinginstitute.stanford.edu/king-papers/documents/why-jesus-called-man-fool-sermon-delivered-mount-pisgah-missionary-baptist
3. Martin Luther King, Jr., *Strength to Love* (Minneapolis: Fortress Press, 2010), 18.
4. King, Jr., *Strength to Love*, 19.
5. Jiddu Krishnamurti, 2nd Public Talk, Bangalore, India, July 11, 1948. https://www.jkrishnamurti.org/content/bangalore-2nd-public-talk-11th-july-1948

Chapter I

1. Hafiz, *I Heard God Laughing: Renderings of Hafiz,* trans. Daniel Ladinsky (Oakland: Mobius Press, 1996), 13.

2. John Welwood, *Toward a Psychology of Awakening: Buddhism, Psychotherapy, and the Path of Spiritual Transformation* (Boston: Shambhala Publications, Inc., 2000), 139.

Chapter II

1. Pablo Neruda, translated by David Whyte in *The Heart Aroused: Poetry and the Preservation of Soul in Corporate America,* (New York: Currency Doubleday, 1994), 96-97.
2. Clifford A. Rickover, *The Stars of Heaven* (New York: Oxford University Press, 2001), xiii.
3. Rumi, *A Year with Rumi: Daily Readings,* trans. Coleman Barks (New York: HarperCollins, 2006), 319.
4. Sharon Salzberg, *Faith: Trusting in Your Own Deepest Experience* (New York: Riverhead Books, 2002), 28.
5. Dennis Linn, Sheila Fabricant Linn, and Matthew Linn, *Healing the Future: Personal Recovery from Societal Wounding* (Mahwah, NJ: Paulist Press, 2012), 3.
6. Ken Carey, *The Third Millennium: Living in the Post Historic World* (New York: Harper Collins, 1991), 84.
7. Frederick Douglass, *Narrative of the Life of Frederick Douglass, an American Slave* (Clayton, DE: Prestwick House Literary Touchstone Edition, 2004), 31.
8. Mary Oliver, *New and Selected Poems* (Boston: Beacon Press, 1992), 110.
9. Tama Kieves, *Inspired and Unstoppable: Wildly Succeeding in Your Life's Work!* (New York: Jeremy P. Tarcher/Penguin, 2013), 20.

Chapter III

1. Rumi, *A Year With Rumi: Daily Readings*, trans. Coleman Barks (New York: HarperCollins, 2006), 58.
2. John Welwood, *Toward a Psychology of Awakening: Buddhism, Psychotherapy, and the Path of Spiritual Transformation* (Boston: Shambhala Publications, Inc., 2000), 275.
3. Welwood, *Toward a Psychology of Awakening,* 277.
4. Sharon Salzberg, *Faith: Trusting in Your Own Deepest Experience* (New York: Riverhead Books, 2002), 38.
5. Salzberg, *Faith,* 47.

6. Patrick D. Miller, "Beyond Belief: Jacob Needleman on God Without Religion." *The Sun,* (December, 2011), 6.
7. Albert Einstein, as expressed to Jost Winteler on July 8, 1901 (CPAE, Vol. 1, Doc. 115).
8. Mary Oliver, *New and Selected Poems* (Boston: Beacon Press, 1992), 94.
9. Ken Carey, *The Third Millennium: Living in the Post Historic World* (New York: HarperCollins, 1991), 177.

Chapter IV

1. Hafiz, *The Gift: Poems by Hafiz the Great Sufi Master,* trans. Daniel Ladinsky (New York: Penguin Compass, 1999), 305.
2. Walter Sullivan, "The Einstein Papers: A Man of Many Parts," *The New York Times* (March 29, 1972).
https://www.nytimes.com/1972/03/29/archives/the-einstein-papers-a-man-of-many-parts-the-einstein-papers-man-of.html
3. Jon Rappoport, Jon Rappoport's Blog. "My Work: The Individual Returns to his Creative Fire," (2017).
https://jonrappoport.wordpress.com/2017/02/24/my-work-the-indi vidual-returns-to-his-creative-fire-4/
4. Dick Cavett, "Bury My Heart on West End Avenue," *NY Times, Op-Ed,* July 11, 2014.
https://www.nytimes.com/2014/07/12/opinion/dick-cavett-bury-my-heart-on-west-end-avenue.html
5. Chris Hedges, *Empire of Illusion: The End of Literacy and the Triumph of Spectacle* (New York: Nation Books, 2009), 103.
6. James M. Washington, ed., *A Testament of Hope: The Essential Writings of Martin Luther King, Jr.* (New York: HarperCollins, 2003), 242.

Chapter V

1. Hafiz, *Love Poems from God: Twelve Sacred Voices from the East and West,* trans. Daniel Ladinsky (New York: Penguin Compass, 2002), 160.
2. Walter Sullivan, "The Einstein Papers: A Man of Many Parts," *The New York Times* (March 29, 1972).
https://www.nytimes.com/1972/03/29/archives/the-einstein-papers-a-man-of-many-parts-the-einstein-papers-man-of.html

3. C.G. Jung, *The Collected Works of C.G. Jung/ Volume 13: Alchemical Studies*, trans. and eds. Gerhard Adler and R.F.C. Hull (Princeton: Princeton University Press, 1967), 265-266.
4. Saki Santorelli, *Heal Thy Self: Lessons on Mindfulness in Medicine* (New York: Three Rivers Press, 1999), 116.
5. Santorelli, *Heal Thy Self,* 109-110.
6. Santorelli, *Heal Thy Self,* 109.
7. John Welwood, *Perfect Love, Imperfect Relationships: Healing the Wound of the Heart* (Boston: Trumpeter Books, 2006), 53-54.
8. Pema Chödrön, *The Places That Scare You: A Guide to Fearlessness in Difficult Times* (Boulder: Shambhala Publications, Inc., 2001), 50.
9. Ram Dass and Paul Gorman, *How Can I Help? Stories and Reflections on Service* (New York: Alfred A. Knopf, Inc., 1985), 220.
10. Sogyal Rinpoche, *The Tibetan Book of Living and Dying*, eds. Patrick D. Gaffney and Andrew Harvey (San Francisco: HarperSanFrancisco, 1993), 200.

Chapter VI

1. Hafiz, *I Heard God Laughing: Renderings of Hafiz*, trans. Daniel Ladinsky (Oakland: Mobius Press, 1996), 113.
2. Nonhuman Rights Project
    https://www.nonhumanrights.org
3. Physicians Committee for Responsible Medicine
    http://www.pcrm.org
4. American Anti-Vivisection Society
    http://www.aavs.org
5. White Coat Waste Project
    http://www.whitecoatwaste.org
6. Rumi, *A Year with Rumi: Daily Readings*, trans. Coleman Barks (New York: HarperCollins, 2006), 164.
7. The website is http://www.cathyginter.com, although that particular content has since been removed.

Chapter VII

1. Hafiz, *The Gift: Poems by Hafiz, the Great Sufi Master*, trans. Daniel Ladinsky (New York: Penguin Compass, 1999), 69.

2. Ken Carey, *The Starseed Transmissions* (New York: HarperOne/Harper Collins, 1982), 46.

3. John Welwood, *Toward a Psychology of Awakening: Buddhism, Psychotherapy, and the Path of Spiritual Transformation* (Boston: Shambhala Publications, Inc., 2000), 138.

4. Pema Chödrön, *The Places That Scare You: A Guide to Fearlessness in Difficult Times* Boulder: Shambhala Publications, Inc., 2001), 42.

5. Carey, *The Starseed Transmissions,* 49.

6. Ken Carey, *The Third Millennium: Living in the Post Historic World* (New York: Harper Collins, 1991), 42.

7. Tama Kieves, *Inspired and Unstoppable: Wildly Succeeding in Your Life's Work!* (New York: Jeremy P. Tarcher /Penguin, 2013), 30.

Chapter VIII

1. Ken Carey, *The Starseed Transmissions* (New York: HarperOne/Harper Collins, 1982), 44.

2. Rumi, *The Essential Rumi*, trans. Coleman Barks with John Moyne, A.J. Arberry, and Reynold Nicholson (New York: HarperCollins, 1995), 281.

BIBLIOGRAPHY

I've read many wonderful books over the years, and all of the authors have added something to my life. They've enlightened me or moved me or provoked me to think and question. Some have brought more tears of joy than others, but all have increased my awareness and lessened my feeling of being alone in the world.

There are some works that, as I read, I can just feel my vibration rising. As I hear the sound of the author's words in my mind, I'm lifted up, my heart is opened with love, and I have hope for humanity. The books in this list are some of these works. They have touched me deeply and have been particularly relevant to the content of the book you're now reading. They are written by authors whose words radiate beauty, and they are food for the soul. I send out a wave of gratitude and love to them as well as to the many authors who've had the courage to let the world see their light in spite of being afraid.

After the review of Ken Carey's *Starseed*, authors are listed alphabetically.

Ken Carey's *Starseed*

The four books of Ken Carey's *Starseed* are *The Starseed Transmissions*, *Return of the Bird Tribes*, *The Third Millennium: Living in the Post Historic World*, and *Vision*. Reading them all was an experience of such utter and unadulterated joy, that I have to say that *The Third*

Millennium and *Return of the Bird Tribes* are the most beautiful books I have ever read. Mere words do not do justice to the experience of them.

In the volumes of *Starseed* the author describes his experience of accessing higher frequencies of awareness, with information flowing to him from angelic consciousness within "eternal fields of light" (*The Third Millennium*, 5) that exist beyond the limitations of the physical realms. This consciousness is also a part of us that we've forgotten. Together the *Starseed* volumes represent "an early translation of the thought circulating in a unified field of awareness that has long been bubbling up through the earth's biology," (*The Starseed Transmissions*, xiv) and provide a preview of future possibilities for humanity. *Vision* presents an overview of planetary evolution and will not be reviewed here.

Carey, Ken. *The Starseed Transmissions*. New York: HarperOne/ Harper Collins, 1982.

The information in this volume deals with the awakening of consciousness, and how our habits of perception have held us back. The words that come through Ken Carey are gorgeous descriptions of how we humans and all of life are individualized expressions of the One, the Creator. But we have forgotten our original essence and have gotten stuck in defining ourselves solely as matter. As we awaken to our true identity as both matter and Spirit, we begin to understand that our bodies are exquisite instruments designed for expressing God in form. "**You** are the Spirit of Life itself, dancing in the clay, delighting in the glorious opportunity of incarnation, exploring the realms of matter, blessing the earth and all therein." (46)

Carey, Ken. *Return of the Bird Tribes*. New York: Harper Collins, 1988.

Before I had even opened my copy of *Return of the Bird Tribes*, I had an experience that presaged its content. It happened late one night while I was swimming alone in a pool on a mesa in Sedona, Arizona. Swimming at night by myself is one of the great joys of my life. Surrounded by water and sky and stars, I feel deeply connected to the source of life, and I go into an altered state that can only be described as bliss. That night as I glided through the water and gazed at the gorgeous expanse of indigo sky pierced by twinkling stars, I kept hearing the words Fire Bird and Thunderbird in my mind. Over and over, Fire Bird, Thunderbird. I had the feeling that the repetition was signifying their importance. Not knowing what the words meant, I filed the incident away and went home a couple of days later. The day after I returned home I picked up my unread copy of *Return of the Bird Tribes*, and as I flipped through the pages I felt a shiver of electricity go through my body. I had spotted the words Fire Bird and Thunderbird together.

They were listed in the Glossary as alternate names for the Great Spirit as well as names of Bird Tribes. I read that the Bird Tribes are angelic entities who have been spiritual guardians of the earth for billions of years. I read further that the White Buffalo Calf Woman, in whose form the Great Spirit had visited the earth to teach the Sioux the ceremony of the Sacred Pipe, said that she was of the Fire Bird tribe. "I am one of the Bird People, whose tribe once covered this Island of the Turtle [North America]. Do you remember the Winged Ones of Heaven? The Firebirds? The Thunder Tribes?" (67) Later on she describes a future time on earth where peace and harmony will reign. "The Great Spirit, the very Thunderbird, will be active within the races, living, breathing, creating through the peoples of the earth." (78)

I was astounded by the synchronicity of my experience, including the fact that Turtle has long been one of my animal spirits, appearing sometimes in my mind when I meditate. I was also truly astounded by the beauty and depth of the words of the angelic Bird Tribes. With love and encouragement they convey to us that they're with us on earth to help us understand our true nature and awaken to our own beauty and power. For example, an angel of the winged tribes tells us,

> "Nowhere but here have I seen such exquisite, sensitive creatures of biology, such graceful men and women who exhibit your capacity. Do not let those of limited vision cheapen the miracle you are living or diminish your sense of value with their abstractions. The potential you embody is unprecedented." (212)

Carey, Ken. *The Third Millennium: Living in the Post Historic World.* New York: Harper Collins, 1991.

Even though the themes of this volume are similar to those in the previous volumes of *Starseed*, I've never responded to a book the way I respond to *The Third Millennium*. When I first read it I had no language to describe all that I felt. Even now, when I reread it, no words can adequately convey the effect that the beauty and magic and energy of this work have on me. The sound of the words and the meaning they carry are so **shockingly beautiful** that with practically every sentence I feel like I'm lifted to a place of transcendence and hope. The angelic consciousness that is with us during this time of awakening comes through these words to help us remember our true, timeless nature and our true purpose—to create worlds through love. Here's an example,

> "If you close your eyes you may see it stretching before you: a pulsing network of implicit potential as real as any sensory realm, a vibrational reality that in an earlier age was called the kingdom of

heaven. ... It is the spiritual scaffold around which the biology of the future will congeal into a work of splendor and magnificence *without precedent and, as yet, without name.* It is a blue-print, a subtle latticework of intent and vibration; it is the outline, the pattern for a finely woven, luminous biology of galactic and someday intergalactic extent. Through you the potential of this implicit order will one day dance to life." (22)

Chödrön, Pema. *The Places That Scare You: A Guide to Fearlessness in Difficult Times.* Boulder: Shambhala Publications, Inc., 2001.

Pema Chödrön, a Buddhist monk, is a gentle teacher, and her book, *The Places That Scare You* is rich with wisdom and compassion. Set within the context of Buddhist teachings, her work deals with some major themes such as mindfulness and using our feelings of pain and confusion as opportunities for spiritual evolving. She suggests that the process of becoming conscious and awake begins with honest and gentle self-observation through which we come to see how we resist the flow of what we feel. We begin to see how we're afraid of experiencing our uncomfortable feelings as they arise, and we see how we create distractions and strategies to avoid staying present with them. As we cultivate compassion for ourselves, in baby steps if need be, we learn to let go of the distractions as well as the stories we tell ourselves about the cause of our pain. We allow ourselves then to experience the bodily sensations of our raw emotions and the living quality of their energy. Here there is no judgment and *no story.* Just awareness.

> "... feeling emotional upheaval is not a spiritual faux pas; it's the place where the warrior learns compassion. It's where we learn to stop struggling with ourselves. It's only when we can dwell in

these places that scare us that equanimity becomes unshakable." (80)

Remaining present and open in the moment to whatever we're experiencing without self-deception takes courage, but with *maitri,* "placing our fearful mind in the cradle of loving kindness," we come to understand who we are beneath our aversions and defenses. We begin to understand that the qualities and behaviors we observe in ourselves and would like to deny are impermanent and not to be regarded as sins. They are,

> "but temporary and workable habits of mind. The more we come to know them, the more they lose their power. This is how we come to trust that our basic nature is utterly simple, free of struggle between good and bad." (75)

Ms. Chödrön gives us some tools to use on this spiritual warrior's path such as cultivating loving kindness and compassion, doing Tonglen, and practicing meditation. Sitting meditation or mindfulness-awareness is a means of developing an unconditional regard for ourselves and for "parting the curtain of indifference that distances us from the suffering of others." (23) Through mindfulness-awareness practice we come to understand our habitual emotional reactions with which we perpetuate our own suffering, and we can then choose to let go of either self-hatred or blaming others.

The author explains that as we learn to not be so afraid of feeling hurt, we can allow whatever pain we feel to soften our heart instead of hardening it. With consistent practice, "We begin to feel some tenderness, realizing that everyone gets caught up as we do and that all of us could be free." (92) As we practice we're led back to remembering our own basic goodness and the basic goodness of all beings, and we are drawn back to the memory that underneath everything we experience, we are already awake.

Dass, Ram, and Paul Gorman. *How Can I Help? Stories and Reflections on Service*. New York: Alfred A. Knopf, Inc., 1985.

How Can I Help? Stories and Reflections on Service is a beautiful, heart-centered work. It's a philosophical, practical, and spiritual exploration of what *really* helps the people we wish to serve as well as ourselves. The authors asked many people who were active in service and social action organizations in America what they considered to be the most important challenges in helping others. Their stories, "living parables," (ix) are deeply honest and human and full of compassion.

As in the Sacred Activism movement, one theme that emerged from their reflections was that to be of real service to others we must know ourselves first. We must know our own resistances and our own fears. The ultimate question that needs to be asked is, "Who *are* we to ourselves and one another?—it will all come down to that." (15) It is through spiritual practice that we come to know ourselves and all beings as Spirit as well as matter. It is through spiritual practice that we realize that being of service to others and ourselves means releasing our sense of being separate from any other being.

> "Here we are then in these forms, helping within our appointed roles, easing the pain of body, heart, and mind, working for peace and justice. And yet in the course of all this, we really *do* go beyond identification with all that would define us as "other." We really *do* meet beyond our separateness. And for however long that lasts, such meeting is what helps ... helps at the level of being ... *is* help

itself. We are sharing the experience of unity. We are walking each other home." (236)

Douglass, Frederick. *Narrative of the Life of Frederick Douglass, an American Slave.* Clayton, DE: Prestwick House, 2004. Originally published in 1845.

Abolitionist, suffragist, author and diplomat, Frederick Douglass has always been a hero of mine. Even before I read his autobiographical *Narrative*, I could feel the goodness of his soul and the depth of his courage just by looking at photographs of him. Reading the eloquent words of his book served to deepen those feelings.

His account of his life as a slave in Maryland and his early years as a free man in Massachusetts is at once gut-wrenching and uplifting. While it's difficult to read of the inhumanity and barbarism of the slaveholders, Mr. Douglass was inspired to use his suffering and that of others to set his path to fight against injustice. One theme of the *Narrative* was his scorn of slaveholding and corrupt, institutionalized Christianity, predominantly in the south. He believed that this version of Christianity did not honor the "the pure, peaceable, and impartial Christianity of Christ." (118)

This work had wide influence and gave inspiration to many in the anti-slavery movement of that time. And it continues to inspire me. From time to time, when I feel afraid to speak about important but unpopular issues, I remind myself of the steely valor and integrity of Frederick Douglass.

Holmes, Ernest. *The Science of Mind: A Philosophy, A Faith, A Way of Life.* New York: Jeremy P. Tarcher/Putnam, 1998.

First published in 1926 and revised in 1938, *The Science of Mind* is an extraordinary work in which the author delineates a theory of universal principles of Reality and how to put those principles into action. When I first read it, the words and their meaning resonated deeply with me as truth. As with all of the books that have been life-altering, I didn't feel as if I were learning something new; rather it felt more like I was having my memory jogged. Stirrings of recognition began to surface.

The premises of the book are simple yet profound and perhaps earth-shattering for those who've never considered them before. In essence, the main points of The *Science of Mind* are:

- that there is a divine intelligence and Spirit that manifests through all of creation, and that "Nature herself is the body of God." (42)
- that we are individualized expressions of this Spirit (or Mind or God or the First Cause).
- that an infinite and immutable Law, acts upon our thoughts and beliefs to bring them into form and manifestation.

The Science of Mind posits that our power to create is the power behind all of creation. When we understand this and attune our thoughts to the Mind of God, we are accessing the unconditional love and creative power of that Mind. In our creating, we need both love and the Law. "Love points the way and Law makes the way possible." (43)

Kieves, Tama. *Inspired and Unstoppable: Wildly Succeeding in Your Life's Work!* New York: Jeremy P. Tarcher/Penguin, 2013.

I remember the first time I picked up the astounding *Inspired and Unstoppable: Wildly Succeeding in Your Life's Work!* I felt as if some kind of etheric lightning were striking my body, awakening some things I already knew but had forgotten. I still feel that way whenever I revisit the book.

Ms. Kieves is an amazing writer. Her anecdotes are so honest and relatable, and often funny; her expansive and joyful presence just radiates through every page. She offers her unabashed and unselfconscious love for us and for life as she asks us to dare to live the life we came here to live. She asks us to dare to pay attention to our dreams that call to us from our Inspired Self. She urges us to let our love guide us more than our fear, and to remember that we are co-creative partners with something higher. In her words,

> "You have the power to work in this world in an extraordinary new way. When you work with inspiration, you work with a *mystical something else*, an Enlivened Presence and Wild Card Intelligence, whether you call it God, Creative Mind, or subatomic nuclear soup." (25)

And,

> "Still, you insist on doubting yourself, calling it 'realism,' to limit yourself to powerlessness. You'd rather 'play it safe,' hedge your bets, trust sweetness only some of the time. But dear one, Wild Visionary people are the new safe. We are agents of invincible faculties. And we're blazing trails of abundance." (18)

Ms Kieves is a great light on the earth.

King, Jr., Martin Luther. *Strength to Love.* Minneapolis: Fortress Press, 2010.

Originally published in 1963, *Strength to Love* is a collection of Dr. King's sermons delivered during the American civil rights movement. Three of them were drafted while he was jailed in Georgia. They combine elements of theology and spirituality, as well as economic and social theory. Taken as a whole the discourses are a beautifully written testament to the principle and practice of nonviolence, seen as God's love in action.

As a Baptist minister he discusses some of the tenets of Christianity in his sermons, but ultimately his words embody a Christ consciousness that transcends any one religion. That consciousness understands that love is the presence that connects all of life and that all life is sacred. His words are essentially a call to Sacred Activism, where we take on injustice without losing our spirit or integrity. That process must begin with our examining our own hearts and minds before we move out into the world to address the moral degeneracy of things like racism, oppression, and the "insanities of militarism" (18).

Strength to Love is one of the books that I look forward to revisiting from time to time. Whenever I read from it, I can feel my vibration rising and my heart opening. I feel I'm in the presence of something holy.

Kinkade, Amelia. *The Language of Miracles: A Celebrated Psychic Teaches You to Talk to Animals.* Novato, CA: New World Library, 2006.

Over the years, I've read some excellent books on how to communicate with animals but none has elicited more unadulterated joy than Ms. Kinkade's *The Language of Miracles: A Celebrated Psychic Teaches You to Talk to Animals.* Her description of her experience with animals from early childhood is uncannily like mine—the insane attraction and love for them, the deep respect for their individuality, and the knowing that animals and humans are deeply connected to each other energetically. Her discourse and stories are so heart-centered and loving, so honest and whimsical and funny that I can't imagine even the coldest heart not melting a little bit while reading this book.

The author suggests that in order to be able to communicate with an animal we need to learn how to tune in to the energetic information already available to us within the unified energy field. Toward that end, she gives detailed instruction on how to begin and deepen the process of talking to animals. All that's needed to start is the desire to connect and communicate. On the philosophical side, she stresses the need for a new world paradigm where spirituality and science "can stand hand in hand, without cruelty, without the misconceptions of the past, recognizing truth while honoring consciousness as fundamental in all living things." (299) Connecting it all to love, ultimately, she states, "I hope you'll love yourself and the creatures around you enough to employ these tools and bless every animal in your pathway." (xx)

Linn, Dennis, Sheila Fabricant Linn and Matthew Linn. *Healing the Future: Personal Recovery from Societal Wounding.* Mahwah, NJ: Paulist Press, 2012.

This is a remarkable, profound, and wise work in which the authors put into words so much of what I've thought and felt for many years. They delineate how our wounding comes as much from the "toxic and insane aspects of our society" (5) as it does from the familial and interpersonal realms. They describe how our culture and our reality have been hijacked by forces that promote an emphasis on violence, cut-throat competition, and the exploitation and destruction of life—human, animal, and environmental—for profit.

Confronting the unpleasant truths about our culture is made difficult by the fact that most of us live in a "media-induced trance." (161) This trance is the result of our being programmed to blindly accept what is presented as truth by media. Another aspect of our being in a trance may come from the fact that societal events can trigger and activate unresolved wounds of our childhood. If we resist facing that inner pain, we'll resist hearing the truth and feeling the pain evoked by world events. Out of fear we may even ridicule and try to silence those who speak the truth.

As the title suggests, the emphasis is on *healing* from this wounding, and the authors use gentle, heart-centered exercises to help us become aware of our inner processes and to help us find consolation in the midst of toxic cultural experiences. Their marvelous stories teach us that we are not helpless or powerless, and that with courage and compassion we can heal our inner and outer worlds.

Pert, Candace B. *Molecules of Emotion: The Science Behind Mind-Body Medicine.* New York: Scribner, 1999.

Molecules of Emotion is a remarkable book. It's the autobiographical work of Dr. Candace Pert, who, as a graduate student at Johns Hopkins University Medical School, discovered the elusive opioid receptor in 1973. She went on to do groundbreaking research into the biochemical basis of our emotions and their central role in health and disease. The findings of her research revealed how our emotions could integrate mind and body through an intelligent, informational, biomolecular network linking the two, and she coined the term "bodymind" to underscore their interconnectedness. She even touched on the need to include the element of spirit into the equation of our health, something she wrote more about in subsequent books such as *Everything You Need to Know to Feel Go(o)d*, 2006, Hay House, Inc., written with Nancy Marriott.

Dr. Pert's fascinating research comes to life in this book, and the science is accessible to non-scientists. She herself comes to life here as well, as she chronicled her journey of challenges, personal discovery, and healing. She is an inspiration and role model for me. How could she not be when she declared her motto to be "Question Authority."

So I was truly shocked and saddened to learn of her untimely death at age 67 in 2013.

Rinpoche, Sogyal. *The Tibetan Book of Living and Dying*, eds. Patrick D. Gaffney and Andrew Harvey. San Francisco: HarperSanFrancisco, 1993.

Sogyal Rinpoche's *The Tibetan Book of Living and Dying* is a masterful work and is considered to be a modern spiritual classic. It's a comprehensive elucidation of traditional and essentially timeless Tibetan Buddhist wisdom. The author's stated goal in writing this book was to expand on the *Tibetan Book of the Dead* by covering life as well as death. "In the Buddhist approach, life and death are seen as one whole, where death is the beginning of another chapter of life. Death is a mirror in which the entire meaning of life is reflected." (11)

The author makes traditional Buddhist teachings accessible to Westerners through the clarity of his writing and the skillful use of wonderful personal narratives, inspiring stories, and literary and scholarly references. He sheds light on such things as the nature of mind and the importance of compassion. One main theme of his work is the value and practice of meditation as the means through which we uncover the nature of the mind in order to "bring the mind home" (57) to the realization of our Buddha nature. "It is meditation that slowly purifies the ordinary mind, unmasking and exhausting its habits and illusions, so that we can, at the right moment, recognize who we really are." (55) There is also an emphasis in the book on shedding light on why the Buddhist tradition places high value in having a spiritual teacher or master in the transmission of the living truth.

> "At the deepest and highest level, the master and the disciple are not and cannot ever be in any way

separate; for the master's task is to teach us to receive, without any obscuration of any kind, the clear message of our own inner teacher, and to bring us to realize the continual presence of this ultimate teacher within us." (134)

The Tibetan Book of Living and Dying gives us inspiration and practical means to live and die consciously. It's a great gift to the world.

Salzberg, Sharon. *Faith: Trusting in Your Own Deepest Experience.* New York: Riverhead Books, 2002.

Faith: Trusting in Your Own Deepest Experience is a profound, gentle, and eloquent book. The faith that Ms. Salzberg writes about is not the blind, unquestioning faith with which some adhere to the dogma of their religion, but the "faith in our innate goodness and capacity to love." (22) Getting to that faith involves learning to trust what our own deepest experience tells us, as well as having the courage to examine our own beliefs. We do these things in order to be more open to a "personal, direct knowledge of the truth." (71) She also encourages us to question what others tell us is the truth. If a teaching resonates with us, we can practice its tenets to see if the results make a difference in our lives. But we must bring the following questions to any belief system including our own: "Can it transform our minds? Can it help reshape our pain into wisdom and love?" (62) Ultimately it is the power of awareness that is within us all that carries us on the journey to this faith.

Santorelli, Saki. *Heal Thy Self: Lessons on Mindfulness in Medicine.* New York: Bell Tower, 1999.

Heal Thy Self is a poignant and life-affirming book about the mutuality and interconnectedness of the healing relationship between health-care professional and patient or client. Its wisdom is not only essential for the helping professional, in their inevitable role of the "Wounded Healer," but is absolutely germane for all of us who wish to become conscious through the crucible of our relationships.

Saki Santorelli, Ed.D, is the director of the Stress Reduction Clinic at the University of Massachusetts Medical Center and is the director of Clinical and Educational Services in the Center for Mindfulness in Medicine, Health Care, and Society. His *Heal Thy Self* contains eloquent essays on such topics as the necessity of becoming mindful in the midst of our distracted lives, the great value of meditation, and the need to pay compassionate attention to our own woundedness before we can truly help another.

Along with the essays is a running account of the eight weekly sessions of one of the courses he facilitates at the Stress Reduction Clinic. This account offers deeply touching stories of the participants' struggles with their illnesses and with their healing, including being asked to enter the terrifying "realm of our broken and unwanted places." (116) Through exercises in mindfulness, participants (and the reader) are asked to gently confront their disowned shadow side, their own brokenness, and to do so without self-recrimination or blame. They're asked to just observe their thoughts and emotions and reactions with a sense of curiosity and an attitude of merely gathering information.

Eventually, through the "nonjudging, nonstriving, generosity-oriented aspects of mindfulness practice" (73) the participants in the course begin to befriend themselves, just as they are. "The feeling of slowly being able to welcome—beyond liking or disliking—whatever entered the field of awareness gave people such relief, hope, and quiet embrace." (73-74) They often reported "a gradual release from the endless cycles of condemnation, denial, justification, guilt, and attempted repentance." (73)

Underscoring the emphasis on the mutuality of the relationship between practitioner and patient, the author offers extraordinary and disarming honesty in the description of his own personal healing journey. And he gives us hope for healing through the motif that runs through the stories and essays in *Heal Thy Self:* that underneath all of the roles we play, like doctor and patient, and all of the self-definitions we cherish and hide ourselves behind, is the memory that no one is truly separate from us.

Welwood, John. *Toward a Psychology of Awakening: Buddhism, Psychotherapy, and the Path of Spiritual Transformation.* Boston: Shambhala Publications, Inc., 2000.

John Welwood writes amazing books. When I first read *Toward a Psychology of Awakening* I was stunned by his masterful integration, at once scholarly and deeply human, of the areas of psychological work, meditative awareness, and spiritual practice. Rereading it years later reminds me of the depth of his vision and compassion. I've long known that talk therapy alone is not enough for healing our whole selves; by itself it bypasses the deeper reality of our spiritual nature. With much wisdom, the author delineates the limitations and pitfalls of using only psychotherapy or only spiritual ideas and practice for healing. For example, he describes the,

> "tendency toward spiritual bypassing—using spiritual ideas and practices to sidestep personal, emotional 'unfinished business,' to shore up a shaky sense of self, or to belittle basic needs, feelings, and developmental tasks, all in the name of enlightenment." (207)

In effect spirituality can end up being just another means of rejecting our raw experience. But Dr. Welwood's work is exceptional in offering the means of merging the spiritual and psychological realms, essentially "integrating our larger nature into the way we actually live." (207)

Yogananda, Paramahansa. *Autobiography of a Yogi*. Los Angeles: Self-Realization Fellowship, 1987.

Sheer joy, from beginning to end. Paramahansa Yogananda is considered to be a Premavator, an "Incarnation of Love," and you can feel his love and wisdom permeating the words and the many wonderful photographs in his *Autobiography*. There's one precious photo of him as a little boy taken around the time that he wrote a letter to God. The image just goes right to my heart. First published in 1946, Paramahansa wrote about all of his life, from growing up in India and his life with his teacher there, to his establishing his Self-Realization Fellowship in California and then around the world. His teachings were a combination of the principles of Hinduism and "original Christianity," with an emphasis on the realization of our divine nature.

I read the *Autobiography* at a low point in my life, and as I read it I had the feeling of coming home to some deep and loving truth, to some kind of safe haven. When I'd finished reading the book, I sat in the lotus position and closed my eyes. I silently offered my profound gratitude and love to Paramahansa for coming to America and for writing his book. With tears of thankfulness and joy welling up in my eyes, I said thank you, thank you. Before I knew it, his beautiful face began to "come together" in my mind, seemingly being put together piece by piece. He smiled at me and I felt a heart connection with him. Soon his image disassembled, so to speak, and he was gone. I felt I'd experienced darshan (a Sanskrit word meaning glimpse or view; an experience of grace and blessing arising from the sight of a holy being). It's an experience I will never forget. Even as I type this manuscript, I just have to lift my eyes to the wall in front of me to see the radiant photo of Paramahansa taken just before his mahasamadhi, a yogi's final conscious exit from the body. I'm still saying thank you, thank you.

Printed in the United States
By Bookmasters